SPIRITED

STOUT BOATS, BRAVE HEARTS

GAIL MASSOTH

KITSAP PUBLISHING

Spirited: Stout Boats, Brave Hearts

By Gail Massoth

First edition, published 2016

Copyright © 2016, Gail Massoth

ISBN-13: 978-1-942661-37-5

All rights reserved. No part of this book may be reproduced or transmitted in any form or by any means, electronic or mechanical, including photocopying, recording or by any information storage and retrieval system, without written permission from the author, except for the inclusion of brief quotations in a review.

Published by Kitsap Publishing
P.O. Box 1269
Poulsbo, WA 98370
www.KitsapPublishing.com

Printed in the United States of America

TD 20160820

50-10 9 8 7 6 5 4 3 2 1

INTRODUCTION

When I worked on the tug, Magic, her skipper Thomas "Skip" Lampman would sometimes get into a mellow story telling mood after dinner at the change of the watch. I don't know if it was the combination of good food and strong tugboat coffee or the soft evocative luster of early evening, but he would settle into his chair behind the wheel in the pilot house, balancing his dessert on his knee and rattle off one story after another. I would prop myself against a bulkhead, sip coffee and travel back in time with him.

As the months went by and Skip continued to spring stories on me, some harrowing and some hilarious, I began to realize that he had amazing recall for details.

The wheelhouse echoed with vivid recollections of his dad, Captain Clarence Lampman, a colorful, accomplished tugboat and ferry skipper who often took Skip, from the time he was eight months old, to work with him. Skip had many miles under his keel by the time he became master of a tugboat at the age of fifteen.

Listening to these fascinating stories, I thought of all the great personal histories that have died with the people who lived them. When I asked Skip if he had written any of this down he looked as if I'd said something outrageous and he said "no," after all he was just telling me about his life. I asked him if he would mind if I took notes, because it seemed such a shame for these stories to just disappear when he stopped telling them.

Once I felt I had wrung every last nuance and detail out of Skip's memory, I wrote everything out and found that I had a substantial amount of material. Throughout his musings were many references to the dogs that accompanied them to work on the tugboats. Skip, seeing that I was really interested in his family, took me through boxes of pictures taken over a period of one hundred years. Then he brought out more boxes of his dad's scrapbooks filled with news clippings of ship wrecks, maritime disasters, and ferry mishaps. Some of the news clippings related to his dad's brother, Harold, a tugboat captain in the San Francisco Bay area, who turned out to be too interesting to ignore.

These men who spent their time on the water and lived to tell about it understood that they must never cloud their perceptions with the illusion of security, with the thinking that everything remains pretty much the same from one day to the next; a concept largely subscribed to by people who live their lives ashore. Change is constant on the water and must be noticed and adjusted to; it is a lifestyle of ebb and flow, learning to use what you are presented with at any given moment.

The view of life from the water is vastly different from that of any other vantage point. All of the irritating intrusions of a crowded, bustling society fall harmlessly away as mooring lines are cast off and the vessel glides into another dimension. The yammering of life's little details is soothed and finally stilled if the voyage is long enough. This is where the soul says "ah." Perhaps this is what lures men back to the sea time after time.

There is a heavy price to pay for this life however; many seamen have expressed a longing to be with their wives and families, they have regretted having to leave, but these men are possessed of unruly spirits that won't allow them the comfort of security and sameness and home; they are driven back to the sea.

I found that being at sea can be a lot like riding an elephant. Much of the time it displays a peaceable gentle disposition, but when it gets rowdy it can hurt you just by its size and power. Watching the welcoming yellow glow of light from the window of a house perched on a tumble of rock on a wild winter night as you hang on while the boat pitches and rolls through storm crumpled seas; the sky a tattered blanket of black sagging overhead, you experience that power. Then comes the morning when the soft sunlight is a benediction and the world around you looks like a religious painting; Jesus light emanating from gilt-edged clouds. Then there are the exquisite surprises; thundering down the Strait of Georgia and being visited by a little bird as it lands on the bulwarks to stop and rest a bit; stepping onto the aft deck at three A.M. just out of the heat and cacophony of machinery in the engine room and seeing a shooting star as though it had waited until you could witness it's passing; standing at the bow of the boat in the middle of the night seeing a brilliant river of phosphorescence as the boat plowed through a huge school of fish.

The nature of tugboats and their work is often reflected in the names men give these boats; Pull and Be Damned, Resolute, Intrepid, Reliable, Stand Fast. A tugboat is essentially made up of a powerful propulsion system and heavy equipment, including a towing winch, surrounded by a sturdy hull which is fendered with thick rubber often in the form of tires. There's not a lot of concession to crew comfort.

The work of towing things on water presents many opportunities for calamity. Inherent in tugboat work is the danger from the equipment itself. Inattentive crew members have been crushed or swept overboard by the towline, smashed by a rampaging barge when it T-bones the tug; killed by a line breaking under tremendous strain. Skipper error has caused tugs to be capsized by their own barges.

Skill and experience are extremely important for the master of a tugboat. It is always pure pleasure to watch someone with natural talent who has honed that gift with the whetstone of practice into a tool of unique grace and usefulness. Give Skip Lampman a tug and a barge and he creates poetry in motion.

I invite you to come along for the ride.

.

CHAPTER ONE

The men on the steam tug, Georgia, were fighting for their lives. Every man aboard the boat was painfully aware that they were not going to make it, thinking any minute now this boat is going to come apart in these seas; we won't see the end of this God-awful day. Clarence Lampman, the mate on the tug, realized with fierce regret that he might not see his wife again.

At midnight on May 30th they had made their way easily through a light westerly swell in the Gulf of Alaska. On the way up the coast they had stopped in Ketchikan on the 27th, where he had sent a lighthearted, teasing postcard to his wife. These could very well be his last words to the woman he was still crazy about after six years together, the mother of their eight month old son.

By 04:00 A.M. on the 31st the wind began to increase, generating choppy seas. The wind steadily continued to build in intensity until, by midday, the storm barreled into them, packing hurricane force winds and monster seas.

Clarence Lampman, normally a skipper, had taken the job of mate on this trip for Shively Towboat Company on the 110' steam tug, Georgia, towing a 240 ton scow loaded with fishing gear from Seattle to Kodiak, Alaska. Three seiners and a floating cannery had headed north with them.

On May 31st they were well into the wide open waters of the Gulf of Alaska when the storm overtook them. They had nowhere to hide. On their port side stretched the heaving tumult of the Pacific Ocean, and on their starboard side, danger of another kind; the rugged Alaska coastline. By 2:00 P.M. they had missed Cape St. Elias and their only hope was to head for Cape Hinchinbrook eighty miles away. The tugboat labored ahead of the huge seas, shuddering as each wave broke over her stern and swept up the deck to the bow.

The men in the wheelhouse were attuned to the boat's response to the strain of the towline as the scow plowed its way behind them through mountains of water. At 8:00 P.M. there was a sudden change in the attitude of the tug as the tension on the towline eased and it no longer knifed through the waves aft. The tow wire had snapped. It was obvious that someone would have to go out on deck, where there was a very real possibility of being washed overboard, to see what the situation was with the towline. If the wire had broken anywhere but right at the tow winch, it would have to be taken in. The threat of the tow wire fouling the propellor drove Clarence and the other mate out onto the plunging deck into the violence of shrieking wind and waves pummeling the tug from stern to stem, waves so high they slapped the top of the tall stack.

They discovered that the towline had parted well aft of the tug, leaving about two hundred feet of cable trailing behind them. When they reached the stern they found that the huge following seas breaking over the aft deck had ripped up a chunk of heavy wooden grating and hurled it around the deck, smashing the steam line that powered the tow winch, making it inoperative. The tow wire had been dogged down, and without the winch they could not slack it off to release it and bring in the broken line. The tail end could not be left to whip wildly in the overtaking seas. It would have to be cut.

The two mates had taken a terrible beating just being on the aft deck, being repeatedly buried by tons of water. In spite of that, they each grabbed one of the axes mounted near the winch, and set to work, bracing themselves to keep from being flushed overboard. Clarence would bring his axe down on the 1 ¼" steel cable as the other mate held his axe under it. As they fought for breath, they were thrown against the deck machinery, smashed into it again and again, as Clarence chopped furiously in an effort to sever the steel wire. In the thirty minutes it took the two men to cut through the cable, they were so severely battered and chilled that they had to have help peeling off their cold, sodden clothes. Clarence had difficulty breathing because of the damage to his back and chest. Some of the crew had to help him climb into his berth where he lay in agony, tossed around by the motion of the boat.

Throughout the deteriorating conditions, Clarence wrote a journal of events in the flyleaf of his British Columbia Pilot, with entries such as "it looks bad for us," and "she can't take much more." Georgia and her despairing crew endured the beating on the eighty miles to Hinchinbrook Island, each man doing everything he could to keep the tug going. Two men labored at the pumps for eighteen hours straight, as the tug writhed in the chaotic seas, her seams opening up, and water poured into her bilges. The engine room crew anxiously attended to the steam engine and its boiler, the usually quiet engine room filled with the din of water boiling past her wooden hull, and the cavitation of the propellor as the tug twisted and gyrated. The skipper and the men in the wheelhouse wrestling the helm hour after hour, wondered how much more of this the rudder could stand before it snapped off and left them adrift to broach and capsize or break apart.

In the dead of the night the skipper found the west end of Hinchinbrook Island, grateful to accept the guidance of the lighthouse beacon and ran four miles along its shore, then turned starboard into the calmer waters of Etches Cove. The men below decks in the engine room, the men on the pumps, Clarence lying battered in his berth, all felt the sudden easing of the tug's motion and knew that they would live to see the sun rise after all. Each man, in his own way said a fervent thank you to the Georgia for getting them to the shelter of this harbor.

Just hours later, though, their dangerously low supply of oil for the steam engine forced them back out into the storm. This time they had some protection from Hinchinbrook and Hawkins Islands as they ran east for Cordova. They found, upon their arrival, that the seiners Fortuna and Rio de Oro, and the cannery, M.S. Commander, had made it to Cordova, but the seiner, Balto, with her four men had not.

While waiting in Cordova for better weather, Clarence bought a postcard of a dog, which he sent addressed to his infant son. "June 2-37, Cordova Alaska. Hello little Skipper. Bet I would like to have you and

Cuddles right here than anything. We have had an awful trip but will soon be heading for home. Bye Bye, Cap"

On June 3, the seas had subsided enough to allow the Georgia to search for the Balto and the scow that had broken loose during the storm. They found the wreckage of the barge on the east side of Montague Island. No trace of the Balto was found that morning as the Coast Guard cutter, Tallapoosa, joined the search. The storm was regaining its intensity so that by mid morning they had to duck in behind Cape Clear on the southwest end of Montague Island. They hove to while they spoke with the Coast Guard crew, who were of the opinion that the Balto had foundered.

By 10:00 A.M. they had taken the Fortuna, which had helped in the search, in tow and ran for the shelter of Latouche Island. After a long day, hammered by wind driven waves, the weary crew reached safety in the lee of Latouche, anchoring at midnight. The following day they were able to make it to Port Ashton, where they waited out a series of storms.

Since the crew of the Georgia no longer had a barge to deliver to Kodiak, they turned around and went home to Puget Sound. On June 12, they pulled into Gig Harbor and took aboard Clarence Lampman's wife, Elsie, and their baby boy, who had come from Port Orchard to meet them. The tug continued working for another eight days with Clarence's family riding along, celebrating his safe return.

Travel at this time in and to Alaskan waters was not greatly enhanced by navigational aids or charts. Clarence was still using his 1920 British Columbia Pilot on his trip in 1937. Mariners were cautioned as follows:

> *"Accuracy of chart – It may, indeed be said that, except in well frequented harbors and their approaches, no surveys yet made have been so thorough as to make it certain that all dangers have been found.*

Large irregular blank spaces among soundings mean that no soundings were obtained in these spots. When the surrounding soundings are deep it may fairly be assumed that in the blanks the water is also deep; but when they are shallow, or it can be seen from the rest of the chart that reefs or banks are present, such blanks should be regarded with suspicion.

Buoys – Too much reliance should not be placed on buoys always maintaining their exact position ...

The light shown by a light buoy can not be implicitly relied on; it may be altogether extinguished, or, if periodic, the apparatus may be out of order." U.S. Hydrographic Office.

In 1900 there were fourteen unlighted buoys on the hundreds of miles of the Inside Passage, and one lighthouse, which was in Sitka, Alaska. That year Congress appropriated funds to build eleven lighthouses on the Inside Passage, and four in southeast Alaska. By 1915 there were three hundred and twenty-nine navigation aids in Alaska, all of which were lighted by acetylene gas beacons. A second lighthouse was built at Cape Hinchinbrook in 1922, the first one having lasted little more than a decade. In 1934 a foghorn was added.

HOONAH, ALASKA IN 1937

CLARENCE LAMPMAN, RIGHT, ON STEAM TUG, GEORGIA

RIO DE ORO, 55', 150 H.P. SEINER

FORTUNA, 36', 35 H.P. GAS SEINER

CHAPTER TWO

The Lampman boys, Harry, Clarence, and Robert grew up on Fidalgo Island in Washington. In 1890 their parents, Frank and Isabelle, had moved from Eau Claire, Wisconsin, leaving behind the small grave of their first born son, Earl, and bringing ten month old Harry west with them. Isabelle's brother, John Hart, moved to nearby Anacortes and owned the steamer, Rustler, which he used for general towing and jobbing.

Clarence was born in August of 1891, at the little community of Dewey, about eight miles south of Anacortes, on the east end of Deception Pass. It was called Fidalgo City at the time, a prosperous lumber village with the island's first commercial sawmill. The settlement had a store, a bank, a saloon, a hotel, and a long dock where up to six boats a day would stop to load wood for their steam engines.

The islanders depended on boats for much of their transportation so it was natural that their children would become adept at running small boats. The Lampman children were no exception, becoming quite skilled in boat handling on the swift, often turbulent waters of Deception Pass.

In 1890, Anacortes sprang from the virgin forest after two thousand acres were cleared in three months, in the belief that this place, with its sheltered harbor, would be perfect for a railroad terminal. In that year, the population mushroomed from twenty-five to over six thousand. By the end of 1890 there were over forty-seven saloons in town. When their dreams of becoming an important railroad hub failed, timber and fishing sustained the town, growing into big industries. Sawmills lined the shoreline, interspersed with canneries that processed salmon and cod; the two largest fish companies being Fidalgo Island Packing Company, and Alaska Packers Association. Steamers and sternwheelers brought passengers and cargo service to the island, taking away canned salmon for delivery to the Puget Sound area and California,

The Lampman family moved to the Ballard area of Seattle in 1906, and Clarence and Harry quickly came up with a plan to make money with their skiff. They would hire out as pilots to bring boats into Salmon Bay through the shifting tide flats. They marked the channel with stakes driven into the mud, adjusting them as the channel changed. Some boat owners did not want to pay for their services, but used the markers anyway. So Harry and Clarence moved the stakes out of line with the deeper waterways, and those who did not pay started to find themselves stuck in the mud. These tactics were effective and the boys were hired again. Clarence made himself fifty cents one day by rowing a passenger to Bainbridge Island, a round trip of at least ten miles. Anxious to get some good boat work, he lied about his age when he was seventeen, in order to get his first master's license.

Harry, a year and a half older than Clarence, succeeded in getting his master's license in 1913, and went to work for Kitsap County Transportation Company, running the 118' steamer, Reliance, from Seattle to Bainbridge Island, with a few other stops in Kitsap County.

From about 1910 to 1912, Clarence lived and worked in an area near Bremerton, known as Manette, where he had a job on the small launch referred to as the Manette ferry. From 1913 until 1917, Clarence skippered a number of small passenger launches around the Bremerton-Port Orchard area. During most of those years, he was employed by the Bremerton Boathouse Company, owned by Captain Martin Heffner, and he ran the launch, Daphne, much of the time. The Daphne's many uses included service as the Soldier's Home Ferry, which ran to Retsil, near Port Orchard.

The Kitsap County Coroner had an arrangement with Captain Heffner's company to pick up and deliver bodies, as the need arose. One day they were dispatched to collect a body at Seabeck, on Hood Canal. Captain Heffner decided to go along on the Daphne for the one hundred mile

THE CREW OF THE KITSAP COUNTY TRANSPORTATION CO. STEAMER, RELIANCE, IN EARLY 1916.

THE LAUNCH, DAPHNE, WITH CLARENCE LAMPMAN ON THE RIGHT.

DAPHNE ON THE WAYS, SKIPPER, CLARENCE LAMPMAN, ON THE FOREDECK.

SEATTLE'S WEST WATERWAY, 1908, JUST NORTH OF SPOKANE ST. BRIDGE. ELLIOTT BAY YACHT & ENGINE CO., FOREGROUND.

IN EARLY DAYS OF TRANSPORTING VEHICLES BY FERRY, THEY WERE LOWERED INTO THE LOWER DECK BY FREIGHT ELEVATOR, TAKING UP TO 45 MINUTES PER CAR TO LOAD.

CITY OF MANETTE, THE LAUNCH USED FOR PASSENGER SERVICE, CIRCA 1911.

DAPHNE, AT RETSIL, ON THE SOLDIERS HOME FERRY RUN.
SKIPPER, CLARENCE LAMPMAN IN THE WHEELHOUSE.

GUNS FROM U.S.S. NIPSIC PRESENTED TO VETERANS HOME NEAR BREMERTON WN.

VETERANS' HOME, AT RETSIL, 1913, FERRY DOCK SHOWING
BETWEEN THE GUNS. BREMERTON IS IN THE BACKGROUND.

trip. By the time they loaded the casket and headed back to Bremerton, it was well into the afternoon. Captain Heffner was feeling drowsy so he went to the forepeak to take a nap. Once he was sleeping soundly, Clarence and the crew quietly jockeyed the casket into position next to him, opened it, and then draped his arm into it next to the body. When he woke, he reacted much like anyone would in these circumstances. To Captain Heffner's credit, he didn't fire Clarence for his prank.

Harry's life was disrupted in the spring of 1917 when the United States entered World War I. He left his wife, Virginia, and their two babies in Ballard, and joined the Navy. He served as an officer until the end of the war in 1918.

Shortly after his return, Harry asked Clarence to come to Alaska with him, and be his engineer on Fidalgo Island Packing Company's boats. Twenty-five year old Clarence decided to take his wife and two young daughters with him on their boat, Olevia L, which he had built for him in Bremerton in 1912.

Several days into the trip from Bremerton, they had just left the northern end of the Strait of Georgia, and were running along the east side of Vancouver Island near Yaculta when Clarence spotted a cannery tender. He pulled up next to them and asked if they would mind if he tied up to them for the night. The crew said sure, they were broken down anyway. Clarence asked them what was wrong, and they told him they couldn't get the clutch to hold, it was slipping so badly. He asked the skipper if he could take a look at it. He worked on the problem into the night, finding that if the clutch had oil on it, it would slip, so he cleaned it up with Bon Ami. He finished the job, satisfied that it worked okay, and went back to his boat to get some sleep.

He awoke to the sound of water rushing by the hull and thought they'd broken loose in the strong current of Discovery Passage. He ran up on deck expecting disaster, and found groceries stacked in the cockpit. They were still tied alongside the tender, which was underway headed north.

THE LAUNCHING OF THE OLEVIAL, 1912, DAPHNE IN THE BACKGROUND.

CLARENCE AND HARRY LAMPMAN ON THE AFT DECK OF THE CELT.

FIDALGO ISLAND PACKING COMPANY'S CANNERY TENDER, THE 70' CELT.

KETCHIKAN, ALASKA, 1917

KETCHIKAN, ALASKA, 1914

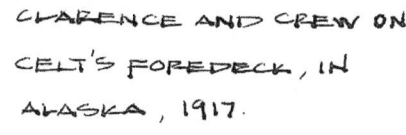

Clarence and crew on Celt's foredeck, in Alaska, 1917.

Towing the Ceres, another cannery tender.

Soupie, the dog

When he and his family arrived in Ketchikan, he went to work aboard the 70' Celt, and the 80' Celtic, 100 h.p. gas powered cannery tenders. At the end of the fishing season, he sold the Olevia L in Ketchikan.

When Clarence left Alaska he relocated his family to Seattle. With the money from the sale of the Olevia L he bought a tugboat and went into business for himself. In his forays along the Seattle waterfront, looking for towing jobs, he made contacts at Drummond Lighterage, a big barge company on the West Waterway. Besides getting work there, he met a man (whose name has been lost) who had a working arrangement with Drummond, as well. Rather than competing with each other for Drummond's business, they formed a partnership.

They added the handsome tug, Rosedale, to Clarence's other slightly smaller tug, Glendale, as they took on more towing assignments. In many instances they would tow a manned barge, loaded with supplies and equipment to remote work sites, such as logging operations that had no dock facilities. Moving the barge into shallow water at high tide, they would run lines ashore, make them fast, and haul up on them with the barge's capstan, bringing it as close into shore as they could. Then they would offload the cargo to the beach, which would lighten the barge, and at high tide they would float it out of the shallows, and be on their way.

Clarence and his partner were getting so much business that they bought another tug for their fleet. The 48' Harold C was a 75 h.p. steam tug built in 1903. They kept her busy towing barges to Bellingham and Ladysmith, British Columbia, on Vancouver Island, to be loaded with coal and brought back to Drummond's terminal on the West Waterway.

While out looking for additional business, someone asked Clarence what the name of his company was. Put on the spot, he said the first thing that came to mind, Seattle Tug and Barge. In the five or six years that he operated his enterprise, he never did come up with a name.

In the mid '20s, Clarence took a job with the Anderson Tow Boat Company of Seattle. Captain Adolph Anderson was a Swede with an entrepreneurial bent, who had a fleet of six tugboats. He and his broth-

er, John, also ran a marine sightseeing tour of Lake Washington, the ship canal, and the locks, on their 90' passenger steamer, Atlanta, which had been built at his brother's shipyard on Lake Washington in 1908.

Clarence ran the 70' steam tug, C.C. Cherry, and the 88' steam tug Anne W, towing, among other things, gravel barges for Pioneer Sand and Gravel Company to Steilacoom and back to their Lake Union Plant. He would sometimes go home in the tug after completing a job, and tie up in front of his houseboat on the ship canal, just around the corner from Lake Union, beneath the University Bridge. On other days he would row to work with the family dog, Tuffy.

Clarence's family life fell apart during his employment with Anderson Tow Boat Co. His wife chose to stay in the houseboat with the children, so he moved out. She also insisted on keeping Tuffy. This was difficult for Clarence, as well as for Tuffy, who was used to going on the boats with Clarence.

This situation really peeved Clarence. When he would go by the houseboat on the tug, in the course of his work, Tuffy would cause a commotion, which aggravated his wife no end. Word of this got back to Clarence, so the next time he went by the houseboat, he blew the whistle. The dog, closed up inside the house, went nuts and blasted through the front window in his frenzy to get outside. He leaped off the dock and began swimming toward the tug. Clarence had to stop and scoop him out of the canal. The incident didn't do much for the already strained relationship with his estranged wife.

The crew of the C.C. Cherry participated in a dramatic rescue when the gas tug, Virginia, exploded and burned at the entrance to the ship canal. They were nearby when the engineer was killed and the captain was blown through the overhead of the wheelhouse, sustaining serious injury. They pulled the badly wounded man from the water and took him to shore, where he could be taken to a hospital.

Clarence happened to be working on the Seattle waterfront on the day early in November of 1927 that the steamship, Margaret Dollar, pulled into the pier with a Japanese sampan in tow. This in itself was

ROSEDALE AND GLENDALE, CLARENCE AND HIS DOG, TUFFY ON FOREDECK OF ROSEDALE. ASAHEL CURTIS PHOTO

Rosedale on West Waterway with a coal barge.
Asahel Curtis photo

unusual, but the story that unfolded was horrifying.

The steamship had come across the Ryo Yei Maru, a Japanese fishing boat, drifting off the Washington coast at Cape Flattery on October 31st. A small boat had been sent over to investigate, and the men found skeletal remains of her crew on the deck. The logbook revealed that the Ryo Yei Maru had departed Misaki, Japan, on December 5, 1926. She had had engine failure several days later. On December 23, she had been hailed by a passing steamship and they had been asked if they would like to abandon their vessel and come aboard. They had declined in the hope that they could get the engine running, or get towed back to Japan by one of their countrymen. But these options never materialized, and the crew died slowly. The Japanese Current eventually carried them to the coast of Washington. Clarence went aboard the sampan once it was tied up alongside a barge. He saw human bones in the stew pot, scattered on deck, and the dried up body of the captain.

TUFFY ON THE BOARDWALK TO HER HOUSEBOAT.

CLARENCE AND TUFFY ROWING TO WORK. PIONEER SAND & GRAVEL COMPANY'S LAKE UNION PLANT IN BACKGROUND.

Anderson Tow Boat Company's tug, Audrey. She was built in 1909, at Tacoma, 65' x 16' x 6.5', for Weeks & Coffman as a steamer to carry freight and passengers.

TUG ANNE W, STEAM BILLOWING OUT OF HER STACK, TIED TO A PIONEER SAND & GRAVEL BARGE.

JAPANESE FISHING SAMPAN, RYO YEI MARU, TIED UP TO A WASHINGTON TUG AND BARGE CO. SCOW ON SEATTLE WATERFRONT, 1927.

CHAPTER THREE

The decade of 1930-1939 had been a time of loss and heartache for many people, after the crash of the stock market in October of 1929. For Clarence Lampman, it began as a time of good fortune. A year prior to the stock market crash, he had gone to work for Puget Sound Navigation Company as mate aboard the ferry Seattle. It wasn't too long before he became the skipper of the Seattle, which ran between Bremerton and Seattle.

One day in the early '30s, Captain Lampman and the mate were people-watching from the bridge as passengers were boarding in Bremerton, when a woman caught Clarence's eye. He pointed her out and said, "See that slick looking blonde down there?"

The mate replied, "You'll never get anywhere with her."

"You want to bet?"

"I'll buy you a hat if you do," said the mate.

Clarence said he'd go down and ask her for a date. Looking fine in his captain's uniform, he strode along the passenger deck seeking her out. He found out that the attractive young woman's name was Elsie, she had a doctor's appointment in Seattle, and yes, she would be happy to go out with him.

Clarence greatly enjoyed wearing that hat.

As the depression wore on, creating widespread joblessness and financial ruin, Captain Lampman had steady employment on the ferries. Deck officers were working up to eighteen hours a day, seven days a week. The crew had days off once a month, but were never allowed

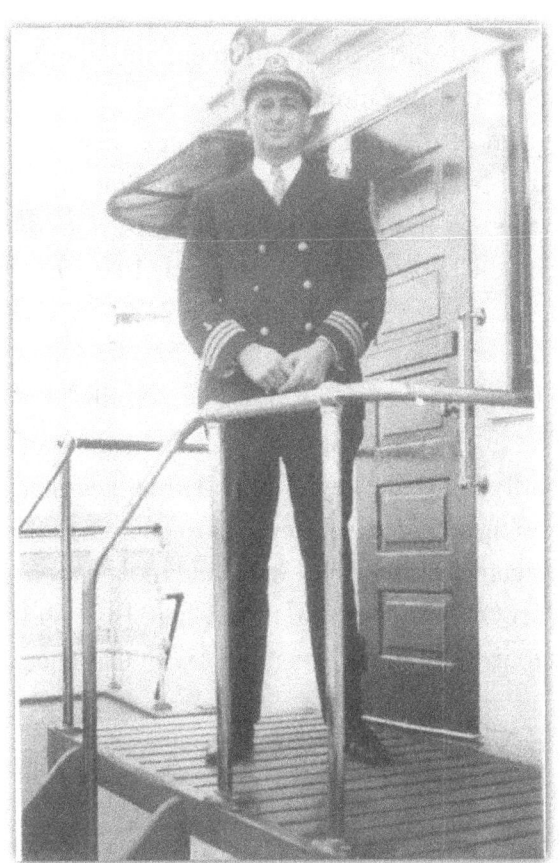

Clarence Lampman in his mate's uniform outside of the ferry, Seattle's, wheelhouse in 1928.

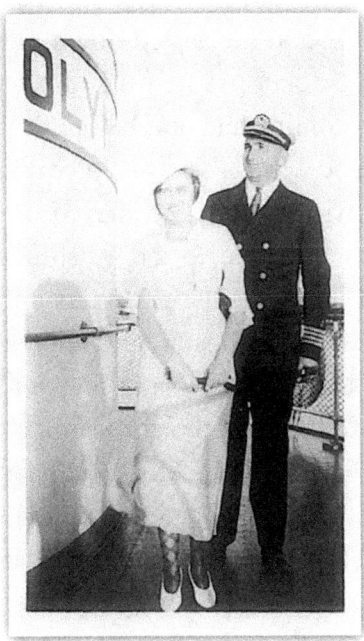

Clarence and Elsie Lampman, August 1933, aboard the ferry, Olympic (formerly Sioux).

more than four consecutive days. Able seamen, firemen, and engine room personnel were paid just over $55 a month.

Seeking relief from the grind of a seven day work week, licensed deck officers from Puget Sound Navigation Company, as well as other inland water companies, applied to the Masters, Mates and Pilots of America Union to start a Seattle Chapter. On December 1, 1931, they became Local #6 and Captain Clarence Lampman was member number six.

Clarence and Elsie were working on a union of their own, finding time to get to know each other and, in spite of Elsie's reluctance to get seriously involved, falling wildly in love. They eventually realized that there was no turning back, and the next logical step was to get married. On February 27, 1932, they became husband and wife, and moved their possessions into a house in Port Orchard, near the farm where Elsie had grown up. They settled into married life, such as it was, with Clarence gone most of the time.

In April of 1932, the Ferryboatmen's Union was chartered, representing all unlicensed employees on inland waters.

Puget Sound Navigation Company's owner, Alexander Peabody, was infuriated by these unions. By June he became fed up with their antics, and he started down the list of MM&P members, firing them one by one. As he worked his way down the list, Clarence saw what was coming and quit before Peabody could fire him, too.

The MM&P Local #6 realized that they were too small to retaliate with a strike, so they chose to boycott Puget Sound Navigation. They appealed to the Washington State Federation of Labor, asking that P.S.N. Co. be put on its unfair labor practices list. It became uncomfortable for union members to be riding unfair boats to and from the Puget Sound Navy Shipyard. The highly skilled members of the MM&P and the Ferryboatmen's Union chartered the Monticello, the old Port Blakely Mill Company steamer, for almost a year, running between Seattle and Bremerton for the Navy Yard workers.

The boycott worked and several of the blackballed officers were reinstated after May, 1933. Even though Captain Alexander Peabody adamantly resisted union demands, by May of 1934 the efforts of the

Captain Clarence Lampman on ferry, Seattle.

S.S. Seattle   Ex. H.B. Kennedy

Seattle, formerly H.B. Kennedy, was built in 1909, at Portland, OR., by Willamette Iron and Steel Co. She was 185' x 28.1' x 11.3', 2000 H.P. steam capable of 21.5 knots under full power. Her name was changed in about 1918.

FERRY RATES
J. S. ROBINSON, Receiver
Edmonds, Washington

Edmonds-Port Ludlow Route
	S.T.	R.T.
Passenger fare	$0.75	$1.25
Autos under 2500 lbs.	2.25	4.00
Autos over 2500 lbs.	2.50	4.50
Motorcycles	1.50	2.50
Auto Trailers	2.00	3.50

Edmonds-Kingston Route
Passenger fare	$0.25	
Autos under 2500 lbs.	1.25	$2.00
Autos over 2500 lbs.	1.50	2.50
Motorcycles	.75	1.25
Auto Trailers	1.25	2.00

Port Gamble-Shine Route
Passenger fare	$0.25	
Autos under 2500 lbs.	1.00	$1.50
Autos over 2500 lbs.	1.25	1.75
Motorcycles	.75	1.25
Auto Trailers	1.00	1.50

Vehicle rates include fare of driver.

Seattle-Port Angeles Thru Stages via Edmonds-Port Ludlow Ferry
Leave Seattle	Lv. Port Angeles
8:00 a. m.	8:15 a. m.
12:15 p. m.	12:45 p. m.
4:15 p. m.	5:00 p. m.

(Over)

FERRY SCHEDULES
Effective May 12, 1923
(Subject to change without notice)

EDMONDS - PORT LUDLOW
Leave Edmonds	Lv. Port Ludlow
5:00 a. m.	6:45 a. m.
8:45 a. m.	10:45 a. m.
1:00 p. m.	3:00 p. m.
5:00 p. m.	7:15 p. m.
9:00 p. m.	10:30 p. m.

EDMONDS - KINGSTON
Leave Edmonds	Leave Kingston
7:45 a. m.	7:00 a. m.
9:15 a. m.	8:30 a. m.
10:45 a. m.	10:00 a. m.
12:15 p. m.	11:30 a. m.
2:15 p. m.	1:30 p. m.
3:45 p. m.	3:00 p. m.
5:15 p. m.	4:30 p. m.
6:45 p. m.	6:00 p. m.
8:15 p. m.	7:30 p. m.
9:45 p. m.	9:00 p. m.

PORT GAMBLE - SHINE
Lv. Port Gamble	Leave Shine
8:30 a. m.	9:00 a. m.
10:00 a. m.	10:30 a. m.
12:30 p. m.	12:45 p. m.
3:30 p. m.	4:00 p. m.
5:30 p. m.	6:00 p. m.

First Class Dining Room Service All hours on Edmonds-Port Ludlow route

J. S. ROBINSON, Receiver
Tel. 881 Edmonds, Main 6906 Seattle

unions had succeeded in reducing the work week to six days a week for the same amount of pay.

Clarence was eventually reinstated as an officer with the Puget Sound Navigation Company, and by 1934 was captain of the ferry Quillayute, on the Kingston-Edmonds run.

Labor trouble continued to rage so fiercely, that in January of 1936, the governor of the state of Washington appointed an arbitration board to set a wage scale for inland boatmen: able seamen's wages rose to $85.50 a month. Ferry service stuttered on through strikes and further arbitration as workers pushed relentlessly for better working conditions. All the while, employers insisted that they could not afford to make the changes demanded of them. The conflict took its toll on relationships, and a pall of acrimony hung over all the combatants.

January, 1936, began a year of changes for the Lampmans. Throughout their four years of marriage, there had been just one sticking point in their relationship, and it was a big one. As their love for each other flourished, Elsie longed to have a child. She was younger than Clarence by fourteen years, and had been a widow when he met her. She had grown up as the middle child in a big, loving Norwegian family, and she was the only one who didn't have children. Clarence, on the other hand, had been married before and had a family, but that ended in divorce, and the pain of that breakup still stung. He didn't care if he ever had another child.

Elsie became pregnant, and her announcement to Clarence rattled him to the core. Not only did he have to rethink his position on the matter, he also had to rein in his apprehension about what this pregnancy would do to her health, which had not been all that robust.

That same year a landslide destroyed the road linking Bremerton and Port Orchard, so Clarence was put on the Beeline, a 93' eighteen car ferry, providing service between the two towns until the road could be rebuilt. Though not a welcome situation for many people, it allowed Clarence to get home to his pregnant wife within minutes after stepping off of the boat.

Capt Clarence Langman

Ferry, Seattle, was rebuilt to carry cars in 1923. She was operated until 1937, then laid up in Winslow. A Luckenback Line steamer is in the background.

Ferry Quillayute in 1934.

In early September Elsie gave birth to a boy, Thomas Harold, the answer to years of prayer. She immediately began her gentle promotion of the child, giving him the nickname of Skipper. Clarence's extreme fondness for his wife overcame his aggravation, so that by the time they came home from the hospital, he had tucked a welcome home present in the baby's crib.

Shortly after the birth of his son, Clarence left the ferries and went back to work on tugboats. Towing companies had not been without their own difficulties, many having been idled off and on through the thirties by loggers' and sawmill workers' strikes. Log towing was a major source of income for tugboat outfits at this time and Shively Towboat Company was no exception.

Clarence did not enjoy being away from his wife, so when the baby was several months old, he asked her to come along on a short log towing job. Elsie packed a bag for the baby with food and diapers, and joined her husband aboard the 60' steam tug, Lumberman. Log towing is never a fast business, but this trip dragged on and on; it was slow even by log towing standards. The diaper supply began to dwindle, dirty diapers piled up, and dense fog dogged them. The fog made it necessary for Clarence to blow the whistle frequently to alert other boats in the area of their presence. Each time Clarence blew the whistle, the baby would jump in alarm and scream. He was soon inconsolable as the ruckus continued, hour after hour. Clarence finally took the baby in his arms, held him up to see the whistle pull, and said "toot, toot." Then he would pull the whistle for a second. Then "toot, toot," and pull the whistle again. Before long, he had his son laughing every time he heard the whistle blow. When the diapers ran out, Elsie washed them by hand and hung them in the engine room to dry, much to the bemusement of the crew.

M.S. QUILLAyUTE.   /5/15/34/

CAPT. C. LAMPMAN.

Puget Sound Navigation Company
50¢   BLACK BALL LINE   ***50¢***

SOUP: PLATE LUNCH: SALAD:
CREAM OF SAPARAGUS.   VEGETABLE.
CHOICE OF: ENTREES:
GRILLED HALIBUT. DRAWN BUTTER.
BRAISED BREAST OF VEAL. DRESSING.
BREADED PORK CHOPS.
FRENCH TOAST WITH JELLy.
HAM, CHEESE OR JELLy OMELETTE.
HOT ROAST BEEF SANDWICH.
              VEGETABLES:
MASHED POTATOES.   HOT PICKLED BEETS.
              DESERTS:
CHOCOLATE PUDDING(15¢) PIE OR ICECREAM(10¢)
      !!!SPECIAL---75¢---DINNER!!!
INCLUDING: SOUP. VEGETABLES. DESERT. COFFEE!
         SPECIAL QUILLAYUTE DINNER STEAK.
    OR   HALF FRIED SPRING CHICKEN.
              *** *******
              A LA CARTE:
ROAST SPRING LAMB. JELLy----------------55¢
TBBONE STEAK. HASJED BROWN POTATOES-----75¢
VEGTABLE DINNER. POACHED EGG------------35¢
POUNDED ROUND STEAK. PAN GRAVy----------50¢
FRENCH TOAST WITH FRIED PINEAPPLE-------40¢
BAKED VIRGINIA HAM SANDWICH. POT. SALAD-25¢
SPECIAL SALAMI SANDWICH. POTATO SALAD--25¢
LIVER SAUSAGE SANDWICH. POTATO SALAD---15¢
COTTAGE CHEESE & PINEAPPLE SALAD-------35¢
COLD DUTCH LUNCH. POTATO SALAD---------50¢
JENNy LIND PANCAKES WITH HONEy---------35¢

DATE   STEWARD   CHEF
        MAX SIEMERS.   CARL LARSON.

CHAPTER FOUR

In November of 1937, after surviving the storm in the Gulf of Alaska on the tug, Georgia, Clarence Lampman left the mountainous seas of Alaska for the mountains of the North Cascades. He was hired by General Construction to run a tugboat at the site of Ruby Dam, a long-planned project of Seattle City Light. Ruby Dam was to be built at the upstream end of Diablo Lake, a reservoir formed by Diablo Dam, which had been built ten years earlier.

Three construction companies merged for the building of the foundation portion of Ruby Dam, and formed the General-Shea-Columbia Company. They needed a tug and two barges on short notice, and realized that they would not be able to use existing vessels because all equipment had to be shipped by train, which involved passing through railroad tunnels.

The man in charge of marine equipment for the project contacted naval architect, H.C. Hanson, to discuss the problem of building a boat and cutting it into pieces in order to deliver it to the remote site. H.C. Hanson had, the previous year, designed and built the first welded, all steel barges for use in Puget Sound and Alaska. He was intrigued with the idea of designing a powered steel vessel. The concept of dismantling it captured his imagination, and he set about designing a boat that could be cut into four sections that could be speedily built at a reasonable cost.

The boat that emerged from the drawing board was 52' long, 15' wide, with a draft of 6'. It was built by Commercial Boiler Works on the Seattle waterfront in seven weeks, and upon completion at the end

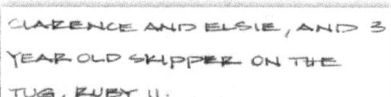

Diablo Camp, set up on Diablo Lake, housed managers and executives, and their families.

Clarence and Elsie, and 3 year old Skipper on the tug, Ruby II.

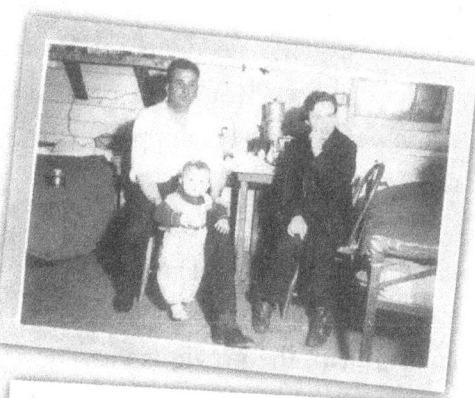

The Lampmans in their quarters at Diablo Camp.

GENERAL-SHEA-COLUMBIA CAMP FOR THE WORKERS, FEB. 1938

SKIPPER ON THE TUG, RUBY II.

THE END OF A LONG DAY. CAPTAIN LAMPMAN STEERING THROUGH AN OPEN WHEELHOUSE WINDOW ON THE RUBY II, TAKING MEN BACK TO CAMP ON ROSS LAKE.

of October 1937, was to be immediately cut into pieces. The house and stack were welded together and taken off as one unit. Double frames were built into the cutting points of the hull. It was determined that cutting off the house and tipping the hull on the railcar would allow them to leave the hull intact. All machinery except the engine was installed prior to dismantling.

At the work site, she was welded back together, the 160 h.p. 4 cycle Washington Diesel was installed, and she was christened the Ruby II. Two barges designed by H.C. Hanson were also built at the job site at the lower end of Diablo Lake, a steel dump barge 112' x 32' with a 340 ton load capacity, and a steel railcar barge, 100' x 32'.

The proposed site for the new dam was a narrow canyon through which the Skagit River swiftly flowed. The volume of water coursing through the canyon could double or triple with little warning. The canyon walls were steep, but the necessary structures had been built to facilitate the work. A skyline had been strung high above the river to move equipment and personnel to the job site. Heavy equipment could be brought in by tugboat and railcar barge and off-loaded onto the skyline. Six hundred feet of railroad track had been laid on the flank of the mountain, and one end inclined at a 68% grade to the river below, where the tug would bring the car barge to the landing. Supplies for the dam site came in by railcar and were loaded, car and all, onto the car barge, towed to the inclined railway and secured to the landing where each car was then hauled up the hill on the track for unloading.

Captain Lampman and the new tug also towed many tons of rock out of the canyon in the dump barge. Logs and debris in the water were a constant hazard to navigation. Much of Ruby II's work was done in narrow channels of moving water, making barge handling tricky, and requiring a skilled captain.

Winter came early to the mountains and stayed late. Temperatures plunged, snow covered earth and equipment, and water froze. To prevent the waterways from freezing solid, Ruby and her crew added ice-breaking to their duties, which had to be done every four hours, day and night, during freezing weather.

There were no roads from the workers' camps to the job site, so men and supplies were transported by the tug. Two camps housed the men; the General-Shea-Columbia camp, near the job site was home to the workers, and the camp on Diablo Lake housed managers and executives, and their families.

In the early months of the dam job, Clarence's wife, Elsie, had made several visits to the camp for Thanksgiving and Christmas, which entailed getting to Rockport and then taking a train to the dam site. By February, Elsie was preparing to close up their Port Orchard house for the move, with their one and a half year old son, to join Clarence at the camp.

Living on her own had presented some logistical challenges. Being short and slight, she had had some difficulties in the hilly terrain of Port Orchard maneuvering the baby carriage by herself. The hill behind the lower part of town rises quite abruptly from the flat shoreline up to a residential area. Their house was perched up on the side of this hill, and it was a struggle for her to get up and down the steep road with the child.

She had started from home down the hill one day, when she lost her grip on the handle of the baby buggy, and it careened down the street in front of the house toward the water below, with her son on board. Elsie had watched in sickened disbelief as the buggy headed for the main street that ran around the base of the hill. The buggy plowed on across traffic, remaining upright, and charged on across level ground until it ran into something and came to a sudden stop.

Little Skipper survived his first solo voyage, with just a small cut near his eye to show for it, and the family reunited at the camp in the mountains. Each family had separate quarters, not houses by any means, but adequate, though rustic, living spaces. The residents created a tight community where friendships were formed by adults and children alike. The snowy settlement was warmed with shared dinners, church and Sunday school, birthday parties, Easter pageants, and the lively presence of children.

Elsie would occasionally walk with Skipper up the Skagit Trail from the camp to the lake, where they would meet Clarence and make the trip back to camp on the Ruby II.

CLARENCE AND CREW ON RUBY II, WAITING AS CAR BARGE IS OFFLOADED AT THE BASE OF THE INCLINED RAILWAY.

CLARENCE AND CREW ON RUBY II, WAITING FOR TIMBERS TO BE LOADED ONTO THE BARGE.

RUBY II TOWING THE DUMP SCOW PAST THE TIED UP CAR BARGE.

RUBY II BRINGING IN LUMBER AND EQUIPMENT.

RUBY II TAKING A BARGELOAD OF ROCK FROM THE DAM SITE.

The men who were at the camp alone lived in bunkhouses. Just after the first Christmas spent at Diablo, the Lampmans received an envelope from one of these men, who had taken some pictures of the family. Where the return address would normally be, he had written "R.A. Maurer, Diablo, In God's Country, without the woman." On the corner where the postage would usually go, he wrote, "Penalty for Private Use to avoid payment of postage, 300 lima beans or 4 sacks of Bull." He addressed it to Mr. and Mrs. Lampman, Yea Man! And Sonny, Too - Somewhere between Diablo and Ruby onboard General Boat – Fergot the name of the durn boat!" He wrote, "Hi Folks, Greetings and stuff – How's tricks and the offspring – Everything "OK" - snow and all we hope ... We still got coffee hyar so effin youalz is down hyar offn on drap in a spell, won't you. We of the Bunkhouse "N" enjoy your company. With the mosta of the besta of New Year's Wishes, Rolly Maurer."

Clarence sometimes took Skipper with him on the Ruby II. Elsie and their son had gone all the way to the dam site with Clarence, as well. The young boy's eyes couldn't travel fast enough around the job site, and he was especially fascinated by the skyline.

The swift, fluctuating current provided a challenge to more than just the tugboat skipper. A tunnel, 27' x 32' had been drilled through the base of one of the canyon walls, the plan being that the river would be diverted into it for the duration of the dam construction. Just downstream from the tunnel, a rock fill was created which partially obstructed the channel, and rock was blasted down from the sheer canyon wall above, in an attempt to block the river and divert the flow. Rising water carried away much of the rock, and the river kept on rolling along. The second attempt, in May of 1938, involved hacking out three holes in the looming rock walls and loading them with explosives. The flow of water was down to 6000 feet per second, so the blast nearly closed the channel, but hot weather brought snow melt roaring out of the mountains, and the river quickly rose to 17,000 feet per second, and swept away most of the material brought down in the second blast.

RUBY DAM AT THE START OF CONSTRUCTION, THE SKYLINE IS VISIBLE.

UNLOADING EQUIPMENT USING THE SKYLINE. THE WHITE LINE IN THE UPPER LEFT CORNER IS THE SKYLINE. THERE IS A PIECE OF EQUIPMENT DANGLING FROM IT, JUST OVER THE BARGE.

A MAN RIDING THE SKYLINE.

RUBY II CARRIED WORKERS SINCE THERE WERE NO ROADS.

RUBY II COMING DOWN FROM THE DAM. WHITE LINE NEAR THE TOP OF PICTURE IS A SURVEY MARK WHICH DENOTES THE HEIGHT OF RUBY DAM WHEN COMPLETED. PICTURE TAKEN FROM COOKHOUSE FLOAT AT RUBY CAMP. (WINTER)

RUBY II PUSHING RAILROAD CARS FULL OF CEMENT.

For the third attempt, old wire rope was threaded through rocks of one to two and a half cubic yards which had holes drilled through them. One end of each cable was anchored to the canyon wall, where the threaded rocks were swept by the force of the river into the channel. The rock wall overhead was blasted, and the fallen rock lodged among the anchored rocks, finally blocking the river bed and forcing the flow into the tunnel. It was a dramatic moment that was covered by the Seattle press.

Clarence's part of the Ruby Dam project was over in two and a half years. A clipping from an unidentified publication sums it up:

"Clarence Lampman, one of the best, has finished up the job at Ruby Dam with the Ruby II. The job was to have lasted six years, but such a fine combination were the skipper, the Hanson-designed tug, and the Washington diesel, that everything was finished sooner."

Diverting the Skagit River. There are men crawling all over the wooden framework. Timber cribs faced with steel sheet piling were placed across the river just upstream of diversion tunnel entrance.

FIRST STAGE OF CONSTRUCTION HALF COMPLETED. THE WAFFLE PATTERN PROVIDED A BOND FOR LATER CONSTRUCTION.

RUBY II IS TIED TO THE CAR BARGE AT THE BASE OF THE INCLINED RAILROAD. THE DUMP BARGE IS BELOW THE DAM. OCT. 1939

CHAPTER FIVE

The spring of 1940 found the Lampman family making an interesting transition from the mountain camp at Ruby Dam, back into the lowlands of Puget Sound. In April, Clarence took his wife and three and a half year old boy to Everett where he had found work on the 53' tugboat, S.S. Goldabell. The employment was contingent on Clarence's ability to get the engine running.

The family had no choice but to move aboard the boat and Clarence spent four days tearing down that lifeless collection of metal parts, and resurrecting it to a state of usefulness. Elsie had her hands full with a restless three year old on a small boat, keeping him out of Clarence's way. The amenities on a tugboat range from modest to nonexistent, and the term "living quarters" would have been a laughable euphemism on a 53' tugboat built in 1925.

After working all day, Clarence fired up the engine at 5:00 P.M., declared it good, and threw off the mooring lines to assist the tug, Nile, in putting thirty-four sections of logs into storage, working until four in the morning. The next day they were on the go, towing two log rafts and picking up gear until 02:30 A.M. of the following day. By 08:00 A.M. they were working at the log storage, and finished by 5:00 P.M. Then it was back to the log storage for another full day. The next morning they moved logs around all day until 5:25 P.M., when the main bearings burned up. So, Clarence tore into the engine again, and their day didn't end until they were towed by the tug, Nile, and finally tied up at 02:15 A.M. of yet another day.

From 08:00 A.M. to seven that evening Clarence labored over the engine, removing all of the main bearings. Parts arrived the next morning, and Clarence worked steadily through the night until 03:30 A.M., when someone from Wilson Machine Works arrived to take out the after main bearing because it was still overheating. They had the engine up and running by 06:45 A.M., and they were off to assist the Nile, tow some boom sticks, grab a raft of logs and tie it up. By 8:30 P.M. they were tied up, letting the bearing cool off. At just after midnight they had made up to four sections of cedar logs and were on their way to the log storage. It wasn't until nine that morning that they tied up to a sheer wall, and everyone collapsed in stuporous exhaustion. By three that afternoon, they were on the move again until midnight, when the current was too swift to tie up their log tow, and so the work dragged on through the early morning until 09:00 A.M.

Just days later they had another bearing failure at midnight while towing eleven sections of logs. They were towed in at 04:00 A.M. by the tug, Siam. Another long day of mechanical work followed. And on it went; one weary day blurring into another.

Working around the log storage, rounding up recalcitrant logs, and corralling them into manageable sections with boom sticks, was not a restful endeavor, even for the family members who were just along for the ride. Bumping the big logs was jarring, the constant shifting from forward to reverse was unsettling, to say nothing of the engine noise. Little Skipper grew increasingly cranky, as sleep deprivation became a major issue in his young life. Elsie lived in daily terror that he would be asphyxiated by engine exhaust while he was in his bunk.

The owner of the tugboats Siam, Nile, and Goldabell was a large, vociferous woman named Dolly Lewis, who spoke in a decibel range not normally associated with human conversation. In June, after two months of nightmarish life aboard the S.S. Goldabell, Clarence called it quits, and moved his family ashore.

CHAPTER SIX

Clarence's abilities as a tugboat skipper soon landed him a job with Pacific Tow Boat Company, under the direction of the irascible operations manager, Louis Moe. He was a short, round, sarcastic Norwegian who had, for decades, overseen the operations of the Everett based company. Clarence and Louis Moe were not strangers to each other, having worked together in the early 1920s. At that time, Clarence had been in charge of tugboat construction at Pacific Tow Boat's Seattle yard. He had lived in a houseboat with his first wife and two daughters below the University Bridge, along Seattle's ship canal.

One day, Mr. Moe, in his customary suit pants, vest, and pocket watch had come aboard the boat that Clarence was working on. He had lost his footing on the deck, and taken a bad tumble that landed him in the water. Clarence hauled him back on board, where he fell unconscious. As he lay splayed out in a sodden heap on deck, Clarence plucked the pocket watch from his vest pocket, and dropped it in a can of kerosene in the engine room.

When Mr. Moe had revived from his ordeal sufficiently, he looked himself over and demanded, "Where's my watch?"

Clarence told him it was in the engine room.

"What's it doing down there?"

"It's in a can of kerosene," replied Clarence.

Mr. Moe went ballistic. But, when he took his cherished watch to a jeweler, he was told that whoever had dunked it in kerosene had saved it. All it required was a good cleaning.

Defender was built in 1900, at Tacoma, for Pacific Tow Boat Co. Her wheelhouse was later cut down to allow her to pass under bridges.

Defender and Sea Vamp tied up in front of the houseboat that was home to the Lampman family.

At the start of construction for the tug, Sea Vamp, in 1923, Mr. Moe had told Clarence to build her according to the plans; no deviations. Mr. Moe was kept busy elsewhere and did not return to Seattle until they had finished the tug. When he came into the yard, he was very surprised to see the graceful, rounded lines of her pilothouse, where he was expecting to see the straight, utilitarian lines of a square house, similar to the one they had put on the Sea Imp the previous year. He asked Clarence about it, and he responded, "You said build it according to the plans and that's what the plans called for." Enough said, end of discussion.

The 55' x 13.7' Sea Vamp, with her 75 h.p., three cylinder Atlas diesel engine, had been put in service to replace the 63' steam tug, Defender. Steam powered vessels throughout the towing industry were being scrapped, sold, or reconfigured to accept the products of diesel technology. Diesel oil had become an attractive fuel alternative at the price of five cents a gallon.

In the early '20s, Clarence had skippered the Defender when he was not occupied with building boats. Log towing provided steady work, as the timber industry flourished, and insatiable sawmills devoured millions of feet of timber.

An element of drama was added to the lives of Clarence and his fellow mariners on Puget Sound, with the onset of Prohibition in 1920. Smugglers of illegal liquor used high-powered boats on the inland waterways to move their product. They would run fast under the cover of darkness, often in close proximity to tugboats, fishing boats, ferries, and cargo vessels.

Clarence's brush with rumrunners came one night out on the sound aboard the tug, Defender, with a big raft of logs strung out behind. At the speed of one and a half knots, the world was passing by slowly and peacefully, to the point of being boring. He had even cut a coffee cup sized hole in the bulkhead separating the wheel house and the galley, so that he wouldn't have to rouse himself to get a refill. Into this somnolent scene came a sleek craft tearing out of the dark right at him. The adrenaline really kicked in when the boat pulled up alongside, and he was told that they needed to make repairs. Suddenly wide awake, he

SEA VAMP TOWING MERRILL AND RING LOGS.

SEA DUKE WAS BUILT AS A PASSENGER BOAT IN 1914, AT MAPLEWOOD BEACH, WA., AND NAMED VICTOR II. SHE CAPSIZED AND WAS RAISED AND REBUILT AS A GAS TUGBOAT BY DELTA V. SMYTH, OF OLYMPIA.

anxiously scanned the water around him for revenuers until they fixed their problem and sped off, leaving him in silence once again.

Once Pacific's new tugboats were completed, Mr. Moe transferred Clarence to Everett to run the brand new Sea Vamp. The Everett crew was a tight group of men who actively excluded newcomers. They took to gathering on the other new boat, the Sea Imp, which had the galley in the fo'c'sle with a skylight overhead in the deck. They would drink their coffee and leave the dirty dishes scattered around the galley when they left. It didn't take long for the deckhand to get tired of cleaning up after them. The deckhand had a glass eye, so one day he said, "Hey, fellas, you might want to look in your coffee cups, I've lost my eye." Those guys never congregated on the Sea Imp again.

When Clarence returned to Pacific Tow Boat in the '40s, the Sea Imp and Sea Vamp were still active in the fleet. He was assigned to the Sea Duke, a boat with an interesting past. She had been acquired by the company in 1924, in trade as partial payment for the tug, Lumberman, which the company had sold to Delta V. Smyth, of Olympia. She was built in 1914 as a passenger vessel and named Victor II. She had capsized and sunk, whereupon she was salvaged by Delta Smyth, and came back to life as a gas powered tugboat.

Clarence had occasion to give that engine a screaming workout. On the Seattle waterfront one day, he saw flames and smoke billowing up from a pier, so he headed over in the Sea Duke to take a look at the situation. He saw that a steamer was tied bow-in to the burning coal dock, helpless to save herself. A frantic crew member on board the ship heaved a line over the stern, down to Clarence, whose instinctive responses kicked into high gear. He made the ship's line fast to the Sea Duke, while the ship's crew threw off the mooring lines that held her close to the flaming dock.

The 61' Sea Duke put her shoulder into it as Clarence advanced the throttle, beginning to ease the bulk of the steamer out of the slip; starting to get a little distance from the blazing structure. As he worked the tug ahead, he grabbed the radio and called Pacific Tow Boat's office to

CLARENCE WITH SKIPPER, AGE 4, UNDER THE STERN OF THE SEA DUKE.

THE COOK ON THE GROUNDED SEA DUKE.

explain the circumstances, and they told him to do whatever he could. So, he pushed the throttle as far as it would go, working the ship out and away, slowly inching it out, giving it everything that engine's 125 h.p. had to give. The ship's stern moved into the open water, and the side of her, amidships, slid through the blistering heat until with maddening slowness, the bow cleared the end of the pier, and Clarence dragged her stern-first out into the bay. In so doing, he redlined the engine and cracked a cylinder head, but he hung on as the ship lowered its anchor. Even as other tugs came out and offered to take the ship, he hung on until she was safely swinging at anchor.

CHAPTER SEVEN

Harry Lampman returned to the ferries after the 1918 trip to Alaska with Clarence. He ran the 145' side wheel steamer, West Seattle, for a short time, and later skippered the 148' passenger steamer, Sioux.

In the 1920s he decided to give California a try, and moved to the San Francisco Bay area. He hired on with Western Pacific Railroad in 1927. By the 1930s Harry was well established with WPRR, where he was captain of the company's tugboats. He moved railroad car barges loaded with freight cars to various ports within San Francisco Bay.

In early 1939, Captain Harry Lampman was happy to have good visibility, especially at midnight on this trip in late January. He was in the Oakland estuary with a steel car barge alongside the tug, Virgil G. Bogue, loaded with ten freight cars carrying canned goods and sand. As he worked his way down the estuary from the Encinal terminals, the 2670 ton freighter, Point Lobos, loomed out of the dark. The frantic sound of ships' whistles pierced the night as the freighter bore down on the tug, pinned against the side of the barge. The huge bow sliced the 170 ton tugboat in half with a terrific grinding crash, as Harry yelled to his crew, "Jump for your lives!" Seven crew members were able to scramble onto the barge. The impact had pushed several men through the tug's galley door. The engineer was able to escape from the engine room through an emergency exit that had been installed just weeks before, crawling out and swimming to the Jacob's ladder hastily thrown over the side of the Point Lobos. The Virgil G. Bogue sank within three minutes, in thirty feet of water, as the lines holding her to the barge parted. The barge began a slow drift to the shore of the estuary where

Probes Ship Crash

Down to a Watery Grave

TUG'S LAST VOYAGE ENDED IN DISASTER

Shown here is the tugboat Virgil C., which was sunk in a collision with the freighter Point Lobos Friday night. The tug sank off Oakland estuary 3 minutes after the crash. The freighter, which figured in "ship murders" of 1936 is due to sail for Port Tampa, Florida. Two crew members who were injured in the crash were reported recovering. Federal officers have begun inquiry.

the Western Pacific sugar dock protruded into the waterway. As the men drifted they assessed their condition, and it was soon apparent that two men were badly injured.

The lighthouse tender on the Oakland side of the entrance to the estuary witnessed the collision, and set out in his boat to rescue any survivors, but everyone was safely out of the water by the time he reached the wreck.

When the barge neared the dock, the crew threw lines over the cleats on the dock and made them fast. They carried the injured men into the railroad yard where a switch engine carried them to a street, where an ambulance met them and sped the wounded men to Merritt Hospital. One man suffered internal and groin injuries, and the other man sustained back injuries, cuts and bruises. Everyone lived to tell about it.

The Point Lobos had been called the "ship murder" freighter, and was considered to be a jinx ship after the engineer was found slain in his cabin three years earlier, on March 22, 1936.

Western Pacific Railroad had been using the 150' ocean steam tug, Hercules, in their car barge towing work since 1924, with Harry as skipper much of the time, and she had been a great boat for the job. So, to replace the Virgil G. Bogue's unsalvageable remains, the company acquired the 150' ocean steam tug, Humaconna, from the Merrill and Ring Lumber Company of Seattle. Hercules had been built in New Jersey in 1907, and Humaconna had been built in Superior, Wisconsin in 1919, each powered by 1000 h.p. steam engines. Humaconna had come around from the east coast in the early 1920s. Both boats had been used to tow massive log rafts of 6,000,000 feet from Astoria, Oregon to San Diego.

Harry divided his time between the Hercules and the Humaconna, both very fine vessels. In the early 1940s, both tugs had their wheelhouses raised to allow their skippers a clear view over the railroad cars on the barges.

Harry became involved in yet another news story on May 14, 1943, when a fire broke out on the San Francisco waterfront. By the time he

Passenger ferry, Sioux, in command of Capt. Harry Lampman, coming out of Burrows Pass for Bellingham. Built in late 1910 for Puget Sound Navigation Co., and put into service early 1911. She was converted to a car ferry in 1923 at Todd Shipyard. In 1924 she was renamed Olympic.

Humaconna with Capt. Harry Lampman in the pilot house.

arrived with the Hercules, the pier was fully involved, creating a tremendous amount of smoke. Several Coast Guard boats were blasting water at the fire as Harry brought the tug into the burning dock to rescue men cut off from shore by the blaze. Pictures in the San Francisco Chronicle captured the drama as it unfolded.

Harry had a similar experience ten years earlier, again in May when the Key System Oakland pier caught fire. Three men, Dispatcher C.J. Rice; train director, Bert Jones, and George Hanson, were on the pier with $6,000 of company cash receipts, and the fire roared through the old wooden terminal building. They had nowhere to go except onto the ferry, Peralta, which was on fire in her slip. Because she was mostly steel, she was slow to burn. The men were forced to the end of the vessel away from the terminal. The fireboat, Dennis T. Sullivan, reached the scene and sent a stream of water onto the Peralta. Harry, on the Virgil G. Bogue, darted in and nosed up to the Peralta and the three men jumped aboard. Within an hour the Peralta was gutted. The Key System's Oakland terminal, the ferry Peralta, and a tug, were all destroyed.

On May 6, at 10:05 P.M., the fire started when hundreds of gallons of fuel oil exploded as it was being loaded onto Peralta. The ferry and the wooden terminal building quickly caught fire and flames raced along 500' of trestle. The explosion happened just as trains were pulling out with passengers from San Francisco. The trains escaped the sudden rush of flames.

There were four ferries at the pier. A ferry that had just unloaded, took another one in tow, and pulled it from the pier. A tug was on the southeast side of the pier, in a repair shop, safe from the fire. There were twenty-two men working on the pier and they all escaped, including the three that Harry saved. Flames were visible for miles, even in San Francisco's Sunset district. The intense heat kept firemen on shore from fighting the fire. Twenty-five m.p.h. winds fanned the fire as it consumed the terminal building, sheds, offices, warehouses, and railroad cars on sidings.

Launches from the Yerba Buena Island naval facility carried marines and sailors to fight the fire from the water. A Red Stack tug towed a ferry clear of the pier and grounded her on a mud flat, not too badly

LOADING RAILROAD CARS AT OAKLAND ONTO THE CAR BARGE.

HUMACONNA AND BARGE #3 ENTERING THE SLIP AT OAKLAND, WESTERN PACIFIC RAILROAD CO.

damaged. There was a very real danger of five storage tanks, containing 10,000 gallons of fuel, exploding as the wind drove flames ever closer. The fireboat, Dennis T. Sullivan, maneuvered in to spray down the tanks in an effort to keep them cool.

The steam ferry, Peralta, gutted down to her hull, had been in service on the Key System San Francisco-Oakland route. Later that year, in October of 1933, she was towed to Seattle by the tug, Creole, after being purchased by Alexander Peabody. Her hull would be the foundation for a famous Seattle ferry, the Kalakala.

Those Lampman boys – drawn like moths to a flame.

Harry's career with Western Pacific Railroad, in the 1940s, included skippering the ferry Edward T. Jeffrey, which carried 2200 passengers across the bay.

CHAPTER EIGHT

Stirrings of unease rippled along the Pacific coast as war news washed over the American consciousness. The population of the western states felt geographically insulated from the rumblings of trouble, but that feeling slowly began to erode as the war drew closer to home. In June of 1940, British Columbia lost a vessel based at the military port of Esquimalt, near Victoria, just across the Strait of Juan de Fuca, in an attack by Germans in the Atlantic. Another of their vessels was sunk in October.

The U.S. Navy was conscripting commercial fishing vessels for patrol duty in Alaska. In 1941, Pacific Northwest boats began showing wartime gray, as company colors were painted over.

The invasion of Pearl Harbor on December 7, 1941, really cranked up the war machine until there was around-the-clock production of vessels of wood and steel. From Bellingham to Olympia, boat yards were soon busier than they had ever been. Even defunct boat building facilities groaned back to life to assist in the war effort.

Unemployment was just a memory, as shipyards sought to attract skilled craftsmen to oversee the throngs of laborers needed in the building of the nation's war fleet. Government contracts were being issued for everything from small tugs, self propelled barges, patrol boats, large tugs and dry docks, to minesweepers, cargo ships, destroyers and aircraft carriers.

The United States was in dire need of ships; having only 7695 at the time of the attack on Pearl Harbor. By August of 1942, the fleet numbered twelve thousand and one as a result of conversion, acquisition,

SKOOKUM, WINSLOW MARINE'S YARD TUG, CLARENCE LAMPMAN AT THE HELM.

and construction. In July, 1943, the U.S. had 20,111 ships of all kinds and by the end of the year their number was 32,179. By February of 1945, the total was 80,522 vessels involved in the war effort.

The threat of America's imminent involvement in the war was a hot topic of conversation across the country, as it certainly was when Clarence and Elsie joined her family's gatherings. Elsie's brother, Ole Lillehei, worked for the Winslow Marine Railway and Ship Building Company on Bainbridge Island, which was gearing up for a big defense contract, as were all of the marine yards around the sound. Ole mentioned to Clarence that they needed a good skipper to run their yard tug.

Clarence became Winslow Marine's yard skipper in charge of the 45' tug, Skookum, in mid 1941. With the Skookum he carried out and serviced the movement of all of the ships in and around the yard. He towed supplies and materials, and fuel, from Tacoma, Seattle, Everett, and Port Townsend. His young son accompanied him on the tug from time to time.

The war years were not easy on the Lampman family. While Clarence was occupied with the rigors of wartime production, Elsie and Skipper were usually left to fend for themselves. Even though they lived on Bainbridge Island, they saw little of Clarence during those years. A deep snowfall during one harsh winter cut them off completely, making it impossible for Clarence to get home and check on his family. He knew that Elsie was made of stern stuff and could handle these challenges, but he was concerned about her health. It was very difficult for him to be away from her; she was the light of his life.

Elsie took her strength of character from her parents, George and Hilbertine Lillehei, who came to the United States in 1903, from Norway. George's family were boat builders and fishermen in the Lofoten Islands. He felt that his brother had the action pretty much sewn up in his hometown, so he decided to look for new possibilities in a new land.

In an open sailboat he had built himself, called a Bindal boat, he and his wife and three small children, and several others who wanted to get to America, set sail across the north Atlantic. The trip was so bad that

ON THE BOW OF THE SKOOKUM, CLARENCE IN THE WHEELHOUSE, WITH WINSLOW MAIZIE AND NAVY PERSONNEL.

GEORGE AND HILBERTINE LILLEHEI CAME TO THE U.S. IN 1903, SAILING AN OPEN BINDAL BOAT ACROSS THE NORTH ATLANTIC FROM NORWAY.

they had to tie one man, who went berserk, to the mast so that he could not jump overboard.

After settling his family in with relatives on the east coast, George went west to set up a home for them in Ballard. They lived there for several years, adding Elsie to the family in 1905.

The industrious George found them forty acres in Fernwood, between Port Orchard and Bremerton, where they established a big, well run farm. They had cows, chickens, a huge vegetable garden, and fruit trees. George, the accomplished boat builder and carpenter, set up his own sawmill and provided well for his family. He brought home salmon he caught in nearby Ross creek.

Their family grew to seven disciplined, hardworking children. They all toiled together, but they loved and nurtured each other as well. The Lilleheis prospered within the community, and in 1913 they became naturalized citizens. But in 1918, when Elsie was thirteen, her father was felled by the Spanish flu, and died suddenly. Without George's driving force, and the income from his sawmill, the two oldest children, Ole and Tudy, had to find work at the Navy Yard.

Much to Clarence's dismay, while he was gone so much because of the war, Elsie became gravely ill, to the point of requiring prolonged hospitalization. Skipper was whisked off to stay with Elsie's sister during the weeks that followed, as Elsie recovered from having her kidney surgically removed. Her upbringing on the farm in an atmosphere of kindness and goodwill, and the sudden, early loss of her father, had instilled in her a strong, resilient spirit that took her physical difficulties in stride.

These weeks, for Clarence, were filled with anguished concern and a sense of helplessness; an unusual emotion for such a capable man.

Winslow Marine accepted a contract to build steel minesweepers, most of which were Raven class, 180', 700 ton, all welded; with the rest being 220' all steel, welded and riveted. Clarence had the added responsibility of piloting the completed vessels during their sea trials. He would take Skipper with him on the days that he ran the sea trials.

The family would do their farm chores, and then clean up for church, walking two miles in their starched Sunday best, to the shore of Sinclair Inlet. They would get into the Bindal boat George had built, just like the ones he had built in Norway, and he would row them across to Bremerton, where they would walk the rest of the way to church.
This picture was taken about 1910.

Elsie Lillehei and her classmates at the Fernwood School.

Winslow Marine had been, since 1916, at the site of the Hall Brothers Marine Railway and Shipbuilding Company, built in 1903, in Eagle Harbor. At the peak of their wartime production, they employed about two thousand five hundred men and women.

Each completed minesweeper, about six a year, had to be put through a rigorous test called a builder's trial. This was a final check to uncover any glitches that might delay delivery of the vessel to the Navy. Shipyard officials and workmen were accompanied by members of the Naval District Trial Board, and the ship's future officers and crew. It was Captain Lampman's job, as pilot, to put the boat through tests of maximum speed, violent turns, reverses, and other maneuvers that would detect flaws in the ship's systems.

After a number of minesweepers had been delivered with no problems, and just before another one was scheduled for sea trials, a naval officer mentioned to Ole Lillehei, Superintendent of Outfitting, that he was of the opinion that the boats were not being fully taken through their paces; that they were being babied. Ole, Clarence's brother-in-law, felt obliged to pass this comment along. Clarence was infuriated.

The night before the builder's trial, Clarence told the engineers to be at the boat by 04:00 A.M. the next day, and to have everything warmed up and ready to go by 07:00 A.M. He wanted the boat to be working ahead on her lines when he stepped on board, with all crew members at their stations. That minesweeper shot away from the dock like a cat with its tail on fire. Boats tied up in the harbor tried to climb up on docks, roll over, and generally chew through their mooring lines in the upheaval of the ensuing Lampman generated tidal wave that morning. After a wild ride, Clarence brought her back to the dock in much the same way he'd left it.

At the end of each successful sea trial, a crew member would run a broom up the halyard to indicate a clean sweep. That broom was up after every sea trial.

One of the first minesweepers completed, in June 1942, was the 220' U.S.S. Pursuit, AM-108, which saw action at Tarawa. Commander Romer Good of the Pursuit, sent Ole Lillehei a Japanese machine gun. He wrote, "Please accept this souvenir from the crew of the Pursuit as

The MINESWEEPER

Voyage I.   WINSLOW, WASHINGTON, JULY 16, 1943   Number 28

Troubled Oceans Call Another Winslow-Built War Craft

Upper left: A tight turn on a trial trip. Looking aft from the searchlight platform the wake tells the tale. The Axis buddies won't approve of this Winslow built ship's maneuverability but our Navy does. Upper right: View of fo'c'sle showing how this sleek craft rides 'em out. "A thing of beauty." Lower left: Navy executives observe activity for'rd. From left to right they are: Lieut. Commander L. H. Hirschy, Capt. H. K. Stubbs, Commander F. F. Sims, Lieut. Commander N. P. Dewrs and Lieut Kermit Newman. The insert (upper right) shows Ole Lillebot, outfitting superintendent, General Manager C. M. Sigle and "Jimmy" Featherstone, general superintendent. Below (left) is "Art" Ayers, vice president of the Company, who operated the engine room telegraph on the return trip, and Captain Clarence Lampman, yard "skipper," who took her out and brought her back.

OFFICIAL TRIAL

AM 111

August 18, 1943

Menu

**WINSLOW MARINE RAILWAY
& SHIP BUILDING CO., INC.**
WINSLOW, WASHINGTON

WINSLOW MARINE RAILWAY & SHIP BUILDING CO., INC.
SHIPS PASS

PERMIT Capt. Longmire
TO GO ABOARD Am-295
1-17-44
DATE   C. M. SIGLE, General Manager

Official Launching Pass
U. S. S. "PURSUIT"
June 12, 1942
WINSLOW MARINE RAILWAY
& SHIPBUILDING CO., INC.
GUEST Thomas H. Longmire

a token of our esteem for you and the workmanship of your people who built the Pursuit ... It is only fitting that you who make such victories possible should receive this gun."

Even as they worked unceasingly to send these boats to the Navy, word arrived that the U.S.S. Salute, commissioned on December 4, 1943, was sunk in June, 1945, as she was sweeping her 144th mine at Brunei Bay on the Borneo coast.

At the end of five and a half years of employment, James Griffiths, president of Winslow Marine Railway, wrote for Clarence, "His services in this capacity were extremely satisfactory and we highly recommend Captain Lampman."

The other Captain Lampman, Harry, did not remain idle during the war. He spent part of the war in Australian waters as the civilian head of merchant shipping. He also served as port captain, at Sydney, Australia, for the Army Transport Service.

On August 6, 1945, Harry's wife of thirty-four years, Virginia died.

Clarence had a friend, Stewart Osborn, who started a column in Pacific Motor Boat magazine, about the goings-on in the commercial towboat fleet, called the Bite of the Line. He called himself Scuttlebutt Pete and wrote in a salty, avast ye maties, style that was well received by hundreds of tugboat men. He did this in spite of being crippled by the advanced stages of arthritis.

In his correspondence with Clarence, which was often illustrated with sketches, he wrote:

"The Lampman Family   January 16, 1943

Dear Shipmates:

Well Christmas is all washed up and put away for another year. I guess it's a good thing that Merry Christmas only comes around once a year because Santa Claus goes off up the chimney, and that's the reason they never had any children they tell me.

Capt. Clarence Lampman in the pilot house of minesweeper U.S.S. Scout during sea trials. Ole Lillehei has his hand on the wheel as his daughter, Mary Lou, who christened the vessel, steers. May 2, 1943

Capt. Clarence Lampman in pilot house of a minesweeper crowded with naval officers during sea trials.

Ole Lillehei, with the Japanese machine gun captured at Tarawa and sent to him by the commander of the minesweeper, U.S.S. Pursuit.

Has Skipper got back down to Earth yet? That little horse just about did the trick for his Christmas. He told me over the phone 'If you think I'm excited you ought to see my father.' Well it sure is a nice present no fooling. I found a road muffin in my stocking. Santa must have left me a pony but he got away ..."

"Lampman Family   February 16, 1943

Port Blakely

Dear Shipmates:

Art Torgeson tells me he has a lady standing the galley watch on the Madrona. Oh well maybe she is just over cautious or with a timidity complex.

And then tugboat men are oh so different sort of brotherly Jetters always so gentle especially when the little gal is heeled with a gat... Your items for the Bite were fine Clarence and I used them all. The skit about Al Ginnette worked up good with a drawing and will appear in the April issue. I think more of those sort of items would liven up the Bite of the Line don't you? The workboat clan are a swell bunch that can take it as dish it out, so a little friendly rib now and then won't hurt anybody.

I'll be sitting on the anxious seat until I hear if you succeeded in getting the lad you had in mind for our next biography ... The thing to do Clarence is to get two or three of these biographies ahead and then I wouldn't have to worry every time wondering if I was going to fail PMB when they are depending on me.

You see this is something new to me Clarence and I guess I've a lot to learn. You and Art are a great help. Without you I would have to fold up and call it a day.

There are so many of the fellows I have never mentioned yet. But after I get established and get this thing to running smoothly mayhap I can get some system to it and get around to all the lads. Your advice keeps ringing in my ears and I am sure you *were right when you said "The more lads you can mention the better and don't forget the Mates, Engineers and Cooks." I am not quite sure I quote you correctly but it was something like that.*

When a fellow is in the pilothouse every tugboat that he passes is a potential item for the Bite of the Line. Just seeing the Mary D. Hume (for an example) with a tow off of Hobo Spit and waving to the genial Captain Gilmore. That's what I mean. There are thousands of items like that around the Sound going to waste every month. For the want of someone to send them to me, you see Clarence most of the lads can't see it for it's too close to them. You are one in a thousand Clarence. You see an item in the most casual meeting.

Well old sock let me know just as soon as you can what's cooking. Love to all the Lampmans."

For Christmas, in 1945, a large group of tugboat men assembled to present Stewart Osborn with a marine radiotelephone that would allow him to keep in touch with everyone.

In the April 1954 issue of Pacific Motor Boat magazine, the editors wrote, "Aye lads, Ol' Scut passed on a bit of a tide ago."

CHAPTER NINE

In 1946, General Construction Company acquired three new tugs. YTLs built in 1945, too late for the war effort; they were Ruby X, XI, and XII. Clarence had run the Ruby II at Ruby Dam for the company and had been considered a big asset to the project.

He hired on with General Construction and was given command of the Ruby XII, 300 h.p., 65' x 17.1' x 6.1'. He would often take Skipper with him, expanding on the teaching he had begun on the tug, Skookum. They made runs from Lake Union to the Mats Mats quarry, and Elliott Bay to Mats Mats with a barge to be loaded with rock. They would get a load of gravel at Steilacoom and take it to Bremerton. They went to Bellingham and Anacortes. On these trips, once the tow wire was let out and the barge was trailing nicely along behind them, Clarence would often turn the helm over to his son, with instructions to wake him at some specific place. For example, if they were taking a barge from Lake Union to Mats Mats, he'd say, "Wake me at Point No Point." Skipper gained a tremendous amount of knowledge and experience on these trips with his dad, who could be an exacting, uncompromising teacher.

Skipper was on a field trip with his class one day, touring the Point No Point lighthouse, when he saw the Ruby XII quite a distance away. He watched as the Ruby XII got closer, working her way into the beach. His dad brought the tug into shallow water, and gave him money to buy everyone in the class ice cream.

The calls to the tug, Ruby VIII, were becoming more urgent, but her skipper did not answer the radio. She had departed from Port Angeles,

CLARENCE ON RUBY XII

RUBY XII WITH A ROCK BARGE, COMING FROM MATS MATS.

SKIPPER STIRRING PAINT ABOARD RUBY XII, AT AGE ELEVEN.

RUBY XII IN THE LOCKS WITH A BARGE.

on the Strait of Juan de Fuca, with an empty barge, and had missed her loading time at the General Construction Company quarry at Mats Mats on Puget Sound, near the entrance to Hood Canal.

On this November day in 1948, other boats in the area were listening to the repeated calls to the Ruby VIII. Among them was the Ruby XII, with Captain Clarence Lampman at the wheel, heading north from the quarry along Marrowstone Island with a barge load of rock, on a course parallel to the one the Ruby VIII had to take to get to Mats Mats. The two boats should have passed each other.

Captain Lampman kept an eye out, scanning the empty waters ahead, to the north, but he had a bad feeling about it. A steady SE wind had settled over the area earlier in the day, pitted against a flood tide pouring in strongly through the strait. Where it made the turn into Puget Sound, the land formed a sharp point, producing a notoriously rough patch of water.

The 65' Ruby XII, with her 300 horsepower, wasn't making a lot of speed, bucking the flood, even staying in close to the beach as Clarence worked the eddies and currents along the Marrowstone shore. He had twelve year old Skipper with him that day, and as they came abeam of the northern end of the island, Clarence gestured ahead to Point Wilson, jutting into the confluence of the strait and the sound, four miles away. There was something off of the point. As they moved closer he told Skipper that it looked like a General barge.

The barge remained stationary, as though anchored in place. Try as they might they could not see the tug. As they finally drew close enough to get a good look, they saw that the tow wire slanted down into the water. The Ruby VIII, about two hundred yards off of the Point Wilson lighthouse, had plummeted to the bottom in 84' of water, taking her crew with her.

Clarence figured that the opposing forces of wind and tide had created turbulent sea conditions, and that the skipper, Captain F.E. Gunderson, had attempted to turn the tug and barge around to get out of it, but she rolled over and sank so rapidly that the skipper and deckhand hadn't had a chance to react. Their bodies were never found.

Just weeks before, Captains Lampman and Gunderson had ex-

Clarence and a General Construction exec., in engine room of Ruby XII.

changed heated words about the seaworthiness of the Ruby VIII. She had been built with a narrow beam to get her through mountain railroad tunnels, and Clarence felt she wasn't enough boat for outside work, especially in the Strait of Juan de Fuca where storms blew up regularly from the Pacific Ocean.

General Construction Company had been so pleased with the performance of the Ruby II during the Ruby Dam job, that they had commissioned the 56' x 14.8' x 6' Ruby VIII. Reliable Welding Works of Olympia, Washington, built her in 1943, during the war years. She worked at the hydroelectric site in the mountains for several years, and then the company brought her out to work on Puget Sound in 1947, where she soon demonstrated her knack for capsizing.

The company raised and repaired her, and put her back to work. In 1960 she was put through inclining tests, which she flunked, so she was hoisted onto a barge and sent to Portland, Oregon, where she was rebuilt. She came out of the rebuild with a sponsoned-out hull and monkey rudders. But it wasn't enough. Ruby VIII towed for a few years on the Columbia River until, in August of 1968, she sank on the Columbia where it joins with the Willamette. This time her crew lived to tell about it.

The ever-restless Clarence joined Puget Sound Bridge and Dredging Company in June of 1949, as skipper of their tugboats, Tom and Jim. He had worked for this company on several projects in the past.

Both tugs headed for Alaska at the beginning of July, with equipment and supplies for a dredging job at Wrangell Narrows. Clarence reached Petersburg aboard the Tom on July 7, and that same day he sent a postcard to his wife. It pictured an Eskimo woman nursing two babies. He wrote, "Arrived Petersburg at noon today. We had a fine trip up. I was sorry to see that my girlfriend wasn't true to me while I was gone, as the picture will prove. We have to go to work, so will write later. With love, Cap."

Clarence held James McCurdy and his dad, Horace W. McCurdy, in high regard. Their company had changed the face of Seattle with such

RUBY II WITH MUD BARGE ON THE DUWAMISH, CIRCA 1945

GENERAL CONSTRUCTION CO. BROUGHT RUBY II OUT OF RUBY DAM DURING THE WAR YEARS FOR USE ON PUGET SOUND. SHE WAS BROUGHT OUT IN PIECES ON TRUCKS, AND THE AIR IN THE TIRES HAD TO BE LET OUT ON THE TRAILER TO GET HER THROUGH THE TUNNELS. RUBY II WENT BACK TO THE DAM AFTER THE WAR, ALONG WITH RUBY VIII. RUBY II STAYED AT THE DAM, AFTER BEING PURCHASED BY THE CITY OF SEATTLE, UNTIL 1959.

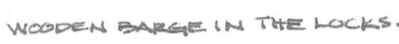

WOODEN BARGE IN THE LOCKS.

feats as the building of Harbor Island and filling in the tidelands separating West Seattle from the city; regrading Beacon Hill; dredging the Lake Washington Ship Canal; among many other projects as far flung as Alaska, Okinawa, and Mexico.

After five months in Wrangell, Clarence conceded defeat. He had to pack up and go home because he was so miserably homesick.

IN 1960, RUBY VIII, WAS TAKEN BY BARGE TO PORTLAND. SHE FLUNKED HER INCLINING TESTS, & WAS REBUILT BY L.S. BAIER & ASSOC., AT WHICH TIME SPONSONS & MONKEY-RUDDERS WERE ADDED. SHE WORKED ON THE COLUMBIA RIVER UNTIL AUG. 1968 WHEN SHE SANK NEAR THE MOUTH OF THE WILLAMETTE RIVER, AT PORTLAND. SHE DID NOT KILL ANYONE THIS TIME!

PETERSBURG, ALASKA IN 1949.

CHAPTER TEN

By the time Skipper, now called Skip, was thirteen, he had years of experience in boats of different kinds. Clarence had seen the raw talent in his son, and given him opportunities to refine that talent where he could keep an eye on him. Clarence had a huge influence on Skip through his instruction, his strong personality, as well as his prolonged absences. Clarence was a hero figure to Elsie, and that constant adulation made a deep impression on the boy. Clarence's abilities and work ethic were greatly respected in the maritime industry. He held himself to a high standard in his work, and expected no less of those around him. His strong work ethic did not necessarily make him easy to be around, but Skip became very capable under his dad's watchful eye.

Each time Skip added another page to his logbook, his confidence burned brighter. Clarence gave his son access to knowledge, teaching him the tricks, juggling a barge, working with lines. Skip logged miles just getting experience, spending time on the boats, absorbing the lessons of wind and water, easing into it as a child with a child's openness and wonder.

When Skip finally received his first paycheck, a lot of water had already passed under his keel. Besides the nautical miles covered with his dad, much of his play throughout his childhood involved boats. He learned to row at the age of four becoming adept at handling a skiff.

Another interest that Skip put a lot of effort into was photography. Elsie's first husband, Tom Turner, had been a professional photographer like his father.

The Turner family had been fond of Elsie, and stayed in touch with

CARLISLE II PULLING INTO THE HORLUCK TRANSPORTATION CO.'S FERRY DOCK, PT. ORCHARD.

THE FAMILY BOAT, SPRAY, 18'6", THAT SKIP TOOK ALONE TO CAPE FLATTERY TO FISH AT AGE 14.

her after Tom's death from brain cancer. They encouraged Skip's interest in photography to the point of giving him a camera, and inviting him to their studio in Bremerton, where he whiled away many enjoyable hours.

Skip landed his first paying boat job on the foot ferry, Carlisle II, as deckhand/purser, for the Horluck Transportation Company. He was friends with Al Lieske, son of the owners Mary and Fritz Lieske. The Carlisle II ferried passengers between Port Orchard and Bremerton.

At that time, Clarence was skipper of the Chimacum, a Horluck passenger ferry, on the evening shift, a position he held for several years, running between Port Orchard and Bremerton.

Later that summer of 1951, Skip went fishing on the troller, Al, off of Neah Bay on the Washington coast, with Fritz Lieske. During the first two weeks of August they caught big, beautiful King salmon on handlines, until Mr. Lieske had caught his fill. Then they headed back to Silverdale.

Skip realized that he could make some excellent money if he could find a way to get back to the fishing grounds. He discussed with his parents the idea of taking the family boat back to Cape Flattery by himself. Clarence displayed tremendous confidence in his son by allowing him to take the 18.6' Spray on the one hundred and thirty mile trip to the Pacific Ocean. There were several older men going out there, and they would cruise in a group.

The Spray had a gas engine, carried 25 gallons of fuel and burned five gallons a day. She had a one burner Primus stove, five gallons of water, a bucket and some life preserver cushions upon which Skip spread his sleeping bag in the forepeak. There was no heat, and her instrumentation consisted of a compass; no radio, and no fathometer.

Handlining by himself, he caught four to five King salmon a day, each about fifty pounds, for which he received fifty-five cents a pound, bringing him about $137 a day. There were days on end when thick fog blanketed the ocean and chilled him, but his compass and his seamanship served him well, and he kept fishing. He found that the fish went through a narrow slot between Tatoosh Island and Cape Flattery on their way to Mukkaw Bay and the Sooes River. As he followed the fish, the swell would pick up his little boat and shoot him between the rocks.

Around Labor Day, Skip gave up fishing and began the trip back home, so that he would be there in time to start school. He had been separated from his dog, Patty, who was usually by his side most of the time. While he was still miles from home, Patty, who was generally well-behaved began acting up during a Labor Day party Clarence and Elsie were having at the house, and she carried on into the evening. At 02:00 A.M. there was no containing her in the house. When Clarence let her outside, she flew down the bank, over the beach and into the water. She heard the Spray's engine chugging up Dyes Inlet, even though Clarence had not yet picked it up. She swam until she came to the Spray, and Skip throttled back and hoisted her out of the cold water, and continued on home with the ecstatic dog. And Clarence and Elsie were able to sleep soundly, once again, with their intrepid boy resting safely in his own bed once more.

Patty, an English Setter, had come out of the woods near their house one day. She was shy and wild, to the point of being feral. She hung around the neighborhood as they encouraged her trust, offering her food and affection. She finally decided that this looked like a pretty good deal so she stayed, on her terms. She would take off on her own from time to time, for days at a time, and all the family could do was wait and hope that she would come back to them. They had grown very fond of her.

When Clarence would go to the wood pile to fill up the firewood box, he would give it to Patty in such a way that she grabbed it, and it would flip over her head. She would walk around with it, bumping into trees and fences, clowning around. Clarence and Skip would be helpless with laughter, which really got her going. If she was hungry, she would pick up her food dish and carry it to the nearest person for a refill.

The following summer, Skip went to work on the Western Star where, after ten days, he was told he couldn't "cut the mustard." With

PATTY DOING HER THING ON THE BOW. WOW.

VIEW FROM SEA DOG'S AFT DECK.

SEA DOG & SEA WEED

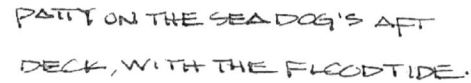

Patty on the Sea Dog's aft deck, with the floodtide.

Patty, dog of the watch, at her usual position at the Sea Dog's bow while under way.

Sea Dog with a log raft in tow.

Patty towing the skiff at the Pt. Orchard log storage.

his ego smarting, he stayed home and rebuilt the family skiff during the month of July. The skiff was named the Floodtide, which, by Clarence's standards was pretty tame: the Fog Auger and the Flying Fudge being a couple of his inventions. The 13.5' Floodtide, with her 4 h.p. gas engine, had been built by Ole Lillehei, Elsie's brother, eleven years earlier in 1941 in Winslow.

Through Clarence's contacts at Pacific Tow Boat Company, Skip made inquiries about finding some part time work. By August 3, he was given command of the tug, Sea Dog, becoming a captain at the age of fifteen.

The Sea Dog was 42' x 9' x 5', built in 1909 and had a 150 h.p. Chrysler Royal, straight 8 gas engine. Boats did not have batteries, so the engine had to be crank started. Skip was hired to run her at the log storage at Gorst. Because he was too young to drive, he used the tug as his transportation to and from work. He would tie her to the mooring buoy in front of the house on Silver Beach, and when he went to work, he would row out in the Floodtide with his dog, Patty, and bring the skiff up onto the aft deck of the tug. He would travel the length of Dyes Inlet and Port Washington Narrows, then take a right to the head of Sinclair Inlet where the logs were stored, which took about an hour and ten minutes each way.

His job was to put together log rafts to be towed by the company's other tugs, to round up deadheads, put away sections of logs that were brought in for storage, and maintain the tugboat. Log rafts were made up using boomsticks, which had a standard length of 66' to 70'. A boomstick went the width of a raft, or boom. Side sticks were boomsticks chained together along the length of the boom. The logs were stowed lengthwise within the boomsticks. At the junction of each side stick, a crosslog, or swifter, was placed widthwise over the top of the contained logs, and chained to the corresponding junction on the other side of the boom. The area in the square created by the swifters and side sticks, about 70' a side, was known as a section. A boom might be many sections long. Log rafts had to be towed slowly, otherwise the logs could roll out from under the boomsticks, or the boomsticks could break. They had to be towed in relatively calm waters.

CAPTAIN OF THE SEA DOG AT THE HELM.

SEA DOG HAULED OUT AT EVERETT.

PATTY, EARS FLYING, IN PORT WASHINGTON NARROWS.

About the only concession to comfort on the Sea Dog was a covered wheelhouse. She had a one burner Primus stove, which Skip brought off of the Spray, and no refrigeration or icebox. There was no head, just a bucket; no sink, no shower. She had a 30 gallon water tank. There was no heater, unless you counted the exhaust pipe that went up through the wheelhouse, so that in summer it added unwanted heat to the small space, and in winter it threw off a paltry amount of warmth.

Skip rigged up an auxiliary power source using an old Briggs and Stratton lawn mower engine of his dad's. It had a one gallon gas tank, and put out fifteen watts. The electrical system was six volts, with a ten watt light in the wheelhouse, a twenty-five watt bulb over the tow bitts, and a light in the engine room.

Rounding up logs was hard, solitary work for a boy of fifteen. Patty kept him company, running on the beach and chasing seagulls. As the tide would go out, Patty would have more beach to run on, which meant that she could get up onto the road. This troubled Skip because he had a great deal of work to do, and couldn't be watching the dog every minute. After mulling it over in his mind for a while, he concluded that by tying a long line to her from the skiff, he would be giving her plenty of running room to terrorize the gulls, while keeping her from being flattened by a car. This arrangement worked very well.

Patty was a smart girl, and as Skip would work his way up the beach, she figured out that she could tow the skiff to him by running on the beach, and swimming where she had to. So they became a team, Skip working the logs, and Patty keeping the skiff close by.

Early in their working relationship, Patty jumped into the Floodtide as Skip was preparing to get underway using the engine. Being an English Setter, she had long tail hairs, or feathers, which this particular morning swished too close to the clutch mechanism, and were yanked into the machinery, stopping the engine. It hurt like hell, especially when she tried to pull free, and she was very unhappy as Skip sawed her tail feather off with his knife, to free her. He made an enclosure for the engine shortly thereafter.

Skip had worked for Pacific Tow Boat only five months when the Sea Dog began to have engine problems. He called Louis Moe at home to tell him about the problem, and let him know he couldn't count on using her until the engine was repaired. Mr. Moe answered the phone, and before Skip could do more than identify himself, Mr. Moe asked, "Where are you? Are you in jail? Do you need bail money?" It was a standard query he made of any of his employees calling him after business hours.

Skip had to take the Sea Dog to Everett for repairs in January, and he had to go up and bring her back later in February, after the engine work was done.

It wasn't long before he was towing logs locally. He also assisted boats, such as the time he helped the Sea Ranger with a 46 section log raft through Rich Passage and around to Port Orchard, then secured everything at the log storage, starting at 05:15 A.M. and finishing late in the afternoon. On one occasion Skip had 128 sections of logs hooked onto the Sea Dog at Port Orchard, and he moved the whole log storage.

One of Pacific Tow Boat's tugs that came regularly to the Port Orchard storage was the 100' George W. She was nicknamed the George Wobbly because her 480 h.p. engine had a tendency to wander a bit. The mounts that attached it to the engine bed had deteriorated so badly that about the only thing holding it in place was gravity. Chains had been installed athwartship to the engine to prevent it from wobbling too much from side to side.

In June of 1955, Skip was assigned to the George W as a deckhand for a few days. Gus Kinnonen, the engineer, was a Finn, and a very nice guy. He had a stool in the middle of the engine room near the engine controls. He would sit with his feet propped up on the base of the engine, with his back resting against a tank.

They were running light (without a tow) to Shelton by way of Hammersly Inlet, an unusually narrow channel, called the Skookum by the locals. The crew had run out of booze, so they were hightailing it into town to stock up. The captain, Virgil Rush, was a cranky, highly excitable s.o.b., but an excellent log man. He would talk very fast and speed up as he became more agitated, until he was impossible to understand. His orders became incomprehensible.

In his tear to get to the liquor purveyor, he ran the boat onto the beach. As the tug fetched up hard on the beach, the George heeled over enough that the engine came up tight on its chain, leaning in the direction of Gus, whose feet were propped in their usual spot on the engine. The tilt of the engine brought Gus's knees up around his ears and pinned him. He couldn't get up, let alone respond to the frantic calls from the wheelhouse to throw her in reverse.

When there was a log spill or other occasion for Pacific Tow Boat to need Skip during school hours, Mr. Moe would call the school and ask if Skip could be excused from class. The school administration always cooperated, and they never marked him absent on those days. This happened half a dozen times a year.

On December 18, 1954, Skip received a call to be at Alki, in West Seattle, at 08:00 the next morning. There had been a log spill around Alki Beach, and Skip was needed to help round up the drifting logs from the broken rafts, as well as beachcomb for the logs that had gone ashore. Clarence drove him to the Sea Dog, which he had left at Port Orchard at 01:00 A.M., and Skip headed for Seattle, not realizing that he had his dad's keys in his pocket. Clarence had to roust his brother-in-law, Rush, out of bed to take him back home to get his spare set of keys.

Patches of fog had begun to form as Skip made his way through Rich Pass. As he entered the open waters of Puget Sound, he stuck the Sea Dog's bow into a dense fog bank. This was Skip's first solo voyage in such conditions outside of the confines of Port Orchard to Silverdale, waters he knew so well.

Skip was running blind, and Patty was no help as dog of the watch. Normally she would ride with her paws on the forward bulwarks of the Sea Dog's bow, with her muzzle resting on her paws. Whenever she would detect something of interest, she would sit up and alertly watch, whether it was a rock, a duck, a boat, or the beach, she was as good as radar, except in fog.

Skip finally heard the Alki foghorn. The gas engine was fairly quiet, so it wasn't too difficult to hear what was happening around the tug. He then picked up the Duwamish Head foghorn. He started to head for Harbor Island, but heard the distinctive whistle of the tugboat, Milwaukee, the last steam tug on Puget Sound. He knew she was big, 107' x 24' x 15.2', and would be towing railcar barges to Port Townsend. He headed back toward the sound of the Duwamish Head foghorn, having seen nothing from the time he had pointed his bow into the murk enveloping Puget Sound. Running carefully along the West Seattle shoreline, he came upon the Phillips Foss, and asked permission to tie up alongside. It was not yet 05:00 A.M., he couldn't go anywhere until the fog lifted, so when the cook on the Phillips offered him breakfast, he gratefully joined him in the warm galley. Patty thought it was a great idea, too.

The fog began to dissipate around 08:00 A.M., at which time Skip began beachcombing. He formed a new raft with the logs he found strewn along Alki Beach, completing it around five that evening. He then had to tow these logs up the Duwamish River a short distance. Having accomplished that, he packed up his gear and headed home, arriving at Silverdale at nine that night.

The whole family was involved in Skip's job. Clarence worked at the log storage from time to time, while Skip was at school, occasionally accompanied by Elsie, who would make the logbook entries. Clarence had left Horluck Transportation after several years, and had gone back to work for the ferries.

By the time he hired on in 1953, Puget Sound Navigation was no longer in the picture. The State of Washington, at the insistence of the public, had bought out Alexander Peabody, after a long struggle resulting from Captain Peabody's disinclination to sell his company. The ferries were no longer run by a private company, and were under the authority of the state government. It was an entirely different work experience. Even the whistle signal was different; no longer one long, and two shorts, and there was a lot of grousing about that by the veteran ferryboat men.

The old Sea Dog was a lot of work to maintain, but Skip tackled every job as it became necessary. He hauled her out and cleaned the

SEA DOG, FORMERLY AUTOMATIC, BUILT IN 1909, 42',
150 H.P. CHRYSLER ROYAL GAS ENGINE.

bottom and changed the propellor. He replaced her exhaust pipe, performed engine repairs and maintenance, and he kept her painted. He received a letter from Mr. Moe – well, actually, his mom did – saying he appreciated Skip's interest in maintaining the boat, and he would send along some paint. The Sea Dog's old engine faltered numerous times between 1952 and 1956, and Skip had to get her to Everett for major engine work, whether under her own power or, as happened in several instances, with her in tow.

The summer that Skip was nineteen, Mr. Moe told him to bring the prop off of the Sea Dog up to Everett with him, while she was dry docked, because the wheels were always getting bent in log storage work. Mr. Moe drove him from Everett to Kennydale, at the south end of Lake Washington, and told him to bring the tug, Thelma O, to Everett. Skip always carried a satchel with clothes and toiletries with him. Upon arrival in Everett with the Thelma O, Mr. Moe said he was going to turn him loose on the Sea Duke. Skip's heartfelt response was that he didn't know anything about the outside boats. Mr. Moe backed off and told him he could ride around with a few people for a while. Then he immediately dumped him on the Sea Duke as captain and sent him with a raft of logs to Tacoma. After that trip, Mr. Moe sent him all over Puget Sound.

Skip called Clarence to see if he had any charts he could use, because there were so few on the Sea Duke. Clarence brought charts to Everett, and Skip fired questions at him the whole time he was there.

One of his first assignments was to pick up a 34 section log raft for Everett. He was then sent off to Port Townsend to pick up a dusty (chip barge) for delivery to Everett. This was his first tow as a captain, and to make matters more tense, the fog rolled in on the trip back to Everett, with the barge drifting in and out of sight through the clinging mist.

Skip called his dad to tell him what was going on. Clarence jumped in his car and drove to Everett. Face to face with Louis Moe, he raised hell and asked him what he was trying to do to that kid? Their heated discussion netted Skip a ride on the Sea Monster as seaman for a couple of weeks.

Pacific Tow Boat had purchased the Sea Monster from the U.S. Navy in 1950. During her renovation before being put into service for the company, she had been equipped with radar at Pacific's yard. The radar had a four inch screen and a range of sixty-four miles. But it took so much power to run that they had to fire up the 30 kW auxiliary, and even that wasn't enough, so they had to use the main engine generator.

During Skip's stint on the Sea Monster, they went to Port Orchard to pick up a log tow from storage. While the raft was being assembled, the captain, mate, and deckhand went up to town to have a few drinks; not an uncommon practice in those days. They stayed way too long at the bar, and staggered back down to the tug. By the time they had gotten themselves sorted out and the raft hooked on, they had missed the favorable tide at Agate Pass. The captain ordered 1500' of tow wire let out, with 48 sections of logs strung out beyond that, and set out for Rich Pass. He turned the helm over to Skip, and he and the other drinkers went to bed to sleep it off.

At Waterman Point, about a mile from the entrance to Rich Pass, Skip called the engineer to say he wanted to take in the tow wire. The engineer told him that they couldn't; he had torn down the auxiliary, thinking he had seven hours to work on it. With no way to take in wire, Skip negotiated the tight bend in the pass by putting the 97' Sea Monster's bow on the far shore and the log raft on the opposite shore. The drunken crew did not leave their berths until they reached Mukilteo, which kept Skip at the wheel for thirty hours without a break.

The cantankerous Louis Moe didn't make Skip's life any easier. In his tirades he was always holding Skip up as an example to the older guys, saying caustically, "I've got this fifteen year old kid that can do anything. I'll get him up here to do it." When Skip came to Everett, they were ready to lynch him. The guys hadn't gotten any friendlier since Clarence's days at Pacific Tow Boat.

One man provided an oasis of goodwill and good sense in the midst of this open hostility. He was Clarence's friend, Joe Budde, the port engineer. His genius with mechanical devices, and his thorough knowledge of every piece of company equipment and their many quirks, kept that fleet of old boats going. He had run the Sea Imp all during World

War II. Skip learned a tremendous amount from him, and appreciated his patient manner. He was a genuinely fine man who greatly influenced Skip.

Another fine person was Louis Moe's wife, Lea. Where he was short tempered and intolerant, she was warm and gracious. One of the company's tugboats, the Lea Moe, was named after this beautiful, elegant woman.

CHAPTER ELEVEN

In the fall of 1955, Skip became a freshman at Western Washington College in Bellingham. He worked his way through school as a tugboat captain, weekends and summers, for Pacific Tow Boat. This meant that he rarely went home. He had had to leave his dog, Patty, with his parents. She would continue to go up to the road and wait for the school bus, as she had done for years, but Skip never got off of the bus. Elsie watched this daily ritual, and would try to coax Patty back to the house.

Skip soon found himself running some of the boats that his dad had built, and later run, in the early 1920s. He spent a lot of time aboard the Sea Imp. She hadn't gotten any more comfortable over the years. The head consisted of a bucket with a toilet seat. Sleeping quarters were crammed in the forepeak with the galley, which had a coil stove and an icebox. In the winter they were thankful that the wheelhouse, at least, had a stove. She had, however, been upgraded in the engine room with a 135 h.p., 900 r.p.m. Atlas High Speed diesel engine, with a Twin Disc clutch with a 2:1 gear. The Sea Imp's aft deck had only five inches of freeboard, so it was awash much of the time, as were the ankles of anyone working back there.

A January storm broke up a raft of logs, strewing its contents along the shoreline of Rich Pass. With the Sea Imp, Skip and the deckhand, Ron Mensinger, were beachcombing and putting the errant logs together into a new raft. Skip was running the Imp and Ron was out on the logs they had rounded up lashing everything together for towing. The Bremerton ferry came through the pass, generating a wake that knocked Ron flat across the slippery logs. His bridgework popped out of his mouth and began a lazy spiral toward the bottom of the channel. Without hesitation he followed his teeth into the water, his mouth snapping on the way down, and that's exactly how he caught them.

Swimming occasionally turned out to be an unforeseen part of the job, as Skip discovered while working logs in Everett. Six boats were taking four sections of logs against a strong current in the river, just managing to hold them in place. All but Skip's towline had been taken off, and it was strung so tight that the logboom was vibrating. There was no way to release it, so Skip went to the stern with an axe to cut it loose. When he hit the wire with the blade of the axe, it whipped violently from the sudden release of tension, the header log it had been attached to jumped twenty feet in the air, throwing Skip without warning into the river. He was pulled under the raft, saw the propellors of the boats turning, shot under the four sections of logs, and was out the other end before he had time to figure out what had happened.

Skip put some time in on the Sea Chicken, a tug that Clarence had run occasionally in 1949. She was 70' x 18' x11', built in 1915 for Pacific Tow Boat, with a Nelseco 4 cylinder, 240 h.p. diesel engine. The Chicken was the first diesel tug in the United States, and the first to have a towing machine. She had, for many years, been named the Chickamauga. On one occasion, Skip had been thrown over the top of the auxiliary while trying to crank start it.

During the summer break from college, Louis Moe told Skip to take a barge up the river in Everett with the Sea Duke. He said, "But Mr. Moe, I don't know anything about the river."

"Hell," Louis said, "kids are out on the river in boats all the time." That was the end of the conversation.

Skip took the barge up the river and succeeded in getting it tied up. By the time it was unloaded, it was two in the morning. He would have to tow the barge, being pulled by the current, through a narrow, unfamiliar stretch of water spanned by numerous bridges.

The guy on the dock told him that the usual procedure for taking

SEA CHICKEN, WITH A LOGRAFT AT PROTECTION ISLAND, STRAIT OF JUAN DE FUCA

THELMA O, AT KENNYDALE, LAKE WASHINGTON

the barge away from the dock was to hook up the head end, which was upriver, and the men on the dock would take off all but one line on the downriver corner of the barge. Skip, he instructed, should then let the current bring the boat and the barge around until they were heading downstream; but not to let it come around too much because it would hit and damage the dock. He warned that they would have to let the line go whether he was ready or not.

So that's what he did, and they were carried along at a pretty good clip, so that pilings that were spaced 80' apart looked like a picket fence going by.

In addition to the Everett and Port Orchard facilities, Pacific Tow Boat Company had log storage at Kennydale, on Lake Washington, near Renton. They kept the 45' tug, Thelma O, tied up at the nearby Scott Pacific dock for the log work there. The Thelma O had been built in 1912 and she was getting pretty creaky by the time Skip ran her. Clarence had condemned her when he worked for the company in the '40s. The engine was so loosely fastened down that, as the shaft spun, the engine would move and water would pour into the bilge. Her nickname was Thelma O Rottencrotch.

Skip was working the Kennydale log storage one day with Floyd Mickelson. To move log rafts, sometimes they would use a maneuver called "the whip," which, if done right, worked very well. On this day Skip did the whip, the Thelma O heeled over, and the pilot house door fell off. This so tickled Floyd that he roared with laughter as they circled back around to fish the door out of the lake.

Summer days along the lake shore could be very warm, and kids liked to play around the log storage. Skip, who was not much older than they were, would chase them off. Some of the boys were not inclined to leave, and Skip would have to insist. In one skirmish he was actually bitten by a surly Renton boy.

In June of 1958, Skip became a tugboat captain with a Bachelor of Arts degree from Western Washington College. He'd found time

Clarence and Skip revisiting Ruby II in the mountains at Seattle City Light's dams on the Skagit River. She remained there until 1959. She was bought by Cotton Construction, Pt. Townsend and named Cotton VIII. She was then sold to Anchor Towing and named Breeze. She then became a research vessel, moored in Poulsbo, and named Discovery. She still has her Washington Diesel.

to be student body vice president and was selected, in his senior year, to appear in "Who's Who Among Students In American Universities and Colleges." This selection was based on "excellence and sincerity in scholarship, leadership and participation in activities, service to the college, citizenship and promise of future usefulness to business and society."

That summer he bought a house near Poulsbo, on Liberty Bay, and moved out of his parent's Tracyton home. Skip went full-tilt into adult life, and in short order he had a wife and a couple of kids.

He still took the Sea Dog to and from work, but he parked her in front of his Poulsbo house, instead of his parents' place. More and more often he ran the Sea Imp which, by 1959, replaced the Sea Dog at the Port Orchard log storage.

One day Skip took a call on the Sea Imp telling him to hurry up and put together thirty-two sections of hemlock logs into a raft and start towing it out of the log storage. He was told that the Sea Roamer would meet him shortly and take over the tow. The sections were made up of very heavy logs, too much for the Sea Imp to tow. Skip expected to encounter the Sea Roamer at any moment as he towed the raft into Puget Sound. The Imp struggled along with the raft until he was off of Mukilteo, about six miles south of Everett, where he called to find out what had happened to the tug that was supposed to relieve him. He was told that her freezer had broken and she was delayed a day, but she'd be on her way soon. Skip told them not to bother because he was already in Mukilteo.

Clarence had not abandoned tugboats altogether, even though he had returned to the ferries years ago. He and Skip found an old wooden tugboat without an engine that they thought they would like to buy and restore. The tug was 48' x 13.4' x 4.5', and had been built originally as a passenger vessel, in 1918. They bought the boat in Port Townsend for $10. Her name was Elk II, and she was in such bad shape that she needed a total rebuild.

This project would also help to restore the father/son relationship that had hit a rough patch. Skip had competed with his dad who had a

SEA IMP HAULED OUT IN EVERETT.

SEA IMP ALONGSIDE A LOG RAFT.

reputation of being an excellent skipper. Skip pushed himself to be better. Clarence had always been a pugnacious guy, so there was bound to be friction between these two strong-willed men.

After many sketches, drawings, layouts, and modifications, they elected to give her a raised foredeck, a gracefully curved wheelhouse, and a stepped down aft cabin and engine room. They could have saved themselves a lot of time and effort if they hadn't gone for the rounded house, but there was no question in their minds about it. Clarence was about seventy when they began this project.

By 1961, Clarence was into his ninth year with Washington State Ferries, eight of those years spent as captain of the 227' Rhododendron, which linked Jefferson and Kitsap counties by providing car ferry service on Hood Canal. Clarence had watched each day as the Hood Canal Bridge took shape; the opening of which would make the Rhododendron's run obsolete. On August 12, 1961, the Rhododendron made her last crossing, easing gently into her slip at Lofall with Captain Lampman at the wheel. He had developed a great fondness for this boat in their years together. Later that day, one week after his seventieth birthday, he retired. He left the Rhododendron to make his last trip on the Klahanie. His wife, son, grandkids, and friends gathered at Kingston to make the final trip to Edmonds with him.

This event was colored by the news he had received a month earlier, that his brother, Harry had committed suicide. He had hanged himself within sight of the last boat he had commanded in his thirty-two years working for Western Pacific Railroad.

Harry had retired in 1959 after running tugboats and ferries, the last of which was the Las Plumas, which was put in service in 1958. She was built for Western Pacific Railroad in Portland, Oregon, and Harry brought her down the coast, when she was completed by Albina Engine and Machine Works.

The Oakland Tribune memorialized Captain Harry Lampman in July, 1961. The paper reported that his coworkers at Western Pacific said he was one of the best known captains on the west coast. He held master's licenses for everything from tugboats to ferries, beginning in 1913. He was involved in many rescues and saved lives many times in

Clarence and Elsie aboard a ferry.

his career, records showed. He skippered boats in Alaska, Washington, Oregon, Canada and San Francisco Bay. He was considered one of the best navigators of Puget Sound waters who ever lived, company officials said. The railroad gave him a special medal for his services.

A few weeks after his dad's retirement, Skip made a big change of his own. He went back to his old high school to teach industrial arts. He continued to run tugboats for Pacific Tow Boat part-time, though, logging as many as seventeen days a month.

In his years at Pacific Tow Boat, Skip worked on nineteen different tugs, working his way up to captain on all but two of them; the Sea Monster and the Sea Horse.

The Sea Ranger was a boat he ran in his years of teaching school. This tug had an interesting history that tied, with an odd twist, to Lionel "Pete" Manning, an industrial arts teacher at Central Kitsap High School with Skip, who had witnessed the following incident. The Sea Ranger was built in 1904, as the Major Evans Thomas, to be a fort tender. She was 105' x 20' and had a steam engine that propelled her at twelve knots. She was put into service at Fort Worden, at Port Townsend, by the U.S. Quartermaster Department. The three forts; Casey, Flagler and Worden, in the northern part of Puget Sound needed something to shoot at for gunnery practice in Admiralty Inlet.

The Major Evans Thomas would tow a target around the bay, and the forts' gunners would pound away at it. In June of 1908, during practice a one pound shell went wide of the target and smashed through the tender's pilot house, just missing her captain, severing the steam line at the boiler, and scaring the daylights out of the Chinese cook.

The Major Evans Thomas retired from Army service, and eventually metamorphosed into a salvage tug, changing appearance drastically several times before settling into her persona as the Sea Ranger.

CLARENCE AND HIS GRANDDAUGHTER, LYNN. HE CALLED HER HIS PRIDE AND JOY.

CAPT. CLARENCE LANDMAN IN THE WHEELHOUSE OF THE FERRY, KLAHANIE, ON HIS LAST RUN BEFORE RETIRING IN AUGUST 1961. ELSIE, SKIP, AND HIS WIFE AND DAUGHTER.

WASHINGTON MOTOR COACH, NORTHERN SHORT ROUTE, AT LOFALL FERRY LANDING, HOOD CANAL.

CHAPTER TWELVE

In one big, sweeping change, Skip cleared the decks and went to work for Foss Launch and Tug Company, ending his eleven year association with Pacific Tow Boat Company, as well as his short teaching career. Going to work for Foss wasn't such a stretch; Pacific Tow Boat had been a subsidiary of Foss for years.

Not long after he left Pacific, the company scrapped four of the boats the two generations of Lampmans had run. The Sea Imp and the Thelma O were stripped of their brass and fixtures, leaned together and torched. The Sea Duke was tied to a quay in Everett and set on fire. The Sea Dog had all of her brass removed and was flattened by a Cat.

After Clarence retired, he and Elsie took a trip east and into Canada, and he told people they were going to cruise on an old tugboat he had fixed up, so it looked like he had retired, but he didn't. He just couldn't do it. Before long, he was back to work on the ferries, sometimes as mate, sometimes as captain. He was on as many different ferries as Skip was on tugs.

Some of the tugboats in the Foss fleet were of even more advanced age than those at Pacific Tow Boat. At Foss, Skip started on the tug, Wallace Foss, built in 1897, for his first four days on the job, in late July, and then he spent most of the month of August yachting. The Foss company yacht, the 65' Lillian D, built in 1905, took three different groups to the San Juan Islands, setting out from Anacortes with Skip as captain.

THE SEA DUKE'S FINAL MOMENTS. MANY WOODEN BOATS WERE DISPOSED OF BY BURNING, THEIR METAL PARTS SCRAPPED OR REUSED.

On their first outing, Skip pulled a Canadian yacht off of Sentinel Island and towed it to Roche Harbor. Then, as they departed Roche Harbor through narrow Mosquito Pass, the Lillian's steering gear conked out and Skip jury-rigged it to get them back to Roche Harbor where he made proper repairs.

His experience running the many boats at Pacific stood him in good stead, because he was assigned to thirteen different boats in fifteen days. For the first five months, he worked mostly in the position of mate, with a few jobs as captain interspersed. After that, he was turned loose as captain, never on one boat for long.

The Foss tugs and their crews were kept busy towing cement barges from Seattle to Bellingham, gravel barges from Seattle to the Steilacoom pit for contracts with Washington Asphalt Company, Glacier Sand and Gravel, and Seattle Ready Mix. There were oil barge runs to Anacortes, Ferndale, and Bellingham, to tank farms in Seattle and Tacoma. And there was ship assist work in Elliott Bay on the Shannon Foss, which worked exclusively at guiding ships into and out of their berths.

In the '60s, Foss kept the old wooden tugs in service, having upgraded machinery as necessary. The Catherine Foss had been the 65' coal burning steam cannery tug Katahdin, built in 1899. She had worked for many years in the fishing industry, and in 1917 began towing logs, which she had continued to do into the early 1940s. She had been repowered in 1930 with a 350 h.p. Union diesel. She still had her engine room controls, and required two engineers, a contributing factor to her layup in 1960.

The Prosper was built in 1898, in Port Townsend, as an 88' passenger steamer for Hastings Steamboat Company. She was turned into a tugboat when Puget Sound Tug Boat Company bought her in 1905. They sold her two years later, and she began towing lumber schooners to and from the lumber mills until 1914, for Admiralty Tug Boat Company. She changed hands a couple of times after that, but stayed in the lumber business towing logs in upper Puget Sound and British Columbia.

Prosper's steam engine was removed and replaced by a diesel, 350 h.p. Atlas in 1934, when she went to Bellingham Tug and Barge Com-

FROM THE 1920S TO THE 1960S, LOG SIZES HAD DIMINISHED CONSIDERABLY.

FOSS'S YACHT, LILLIAN D, IN THE SAN JUAN ISLANDS.

pany. Like many other boats she was conscripted into military service, and her company colors painted over with gray, by the Army from 1942 until the end of World War II in 1945, at which time she was returned to Bellingham Tug and Barge, which had become a Foss subsidiary. She was transferred to Foss in 1960.

The Anna Foss was built at Tacoma as a 69' x 18', 75 h.p. steam tug in 1907. She started out as the Vigilant, a name she kept until 1933, when she was bought at Marshall's auction by Foss. She had been re-powered to diesel in the twenties, and Foss upgraded her to a 300 h.p. Enterprise in 1938.

The 58' Wallace Foss was built in 1897, at Tacoma, and named the Oscar B. She had been powered with a 100 h.p. steam engine. Her name was changed to Rouse when she was bought by Rouse Towing Company. When Foss Launch and Tug purchased Rouse Towing, she was rebuilt and repowered several times over the years. In 1960 she had been refurbished yet again, and given a 230 h.p. Caterpillar diesel.

Although the majority of the work at Foss was accomplished using barges, Skip didn't get completely away from log towing. Log rafts had changed a great deal from the time that Skip had ridden on his dad's tugs, to the mid-sixties. Clarence had towed 16 to 20 sections of huge logs with the 135 h.p. Sea Vamp. Skip had towed 32 to 48 sections of big logs with 300 h.p. The biggest logs he had ever towed, he'd had to scale in order to get on top of them to walk around and count them; there had been thirty logs in four sections. He had seen sections go from forty logs, to sixty, to eighty and finally, one hundred and twenty logs, as trees available for cutting became smaller and smaller.

In late August of 1964, Skip had been on the tug, Prosper, for six days, and he was on his way from Port Angeles with a log tow of forty to fifty sections. There were two tugs on the raft; the Sea Chicken was on the front end because she was going to take it all the way in to Everett. The Prosper was assigned to assist the Chicken in the Strait of Juan de Fuca, and around through the northern part of Puget Sound. They had rounded Point Wilson and were almost abeam of Marrowstone

light. Skip went out on the log raft to move the towline. The raft consisted of small logs that had been in the water for a long time. While he was trying to jump from one bundle to the next, the water-soaked bark slipped off of the log when Skip's foot hit it. He landed badly and his leg snapped, causing him to lose his balance and fall off of the raft into the water. He dragged himself back up on the logs. The mate on the Prosper saw that Skip was in trouble and called the Coast Guard. They had a cutter just two miles away, but they decided to send a helicopter from Port Angeles instead. It took an hour for the helicopter to reach them, while Skip lay sprawled on the logs, soaking wet and chilled, in agony with a horribly fractured tibia jutting through the skin of his lower leg.

When the Coast Guard arrived, they lowered a basket stretcher which just missed Skip's head. He reached out to steady it and the static electricity from it knocked him off of the logs and into the water. While he was in the water, they worked the stretcher over to him and he was able to grab it and roll into it, the pain from his broken leg sickening.

They took him to Port Townsend where they set the helicopter down in an orchard and called an ambulance. When the ambulance arrived, he was bundled into it, wet and bleeding, and rushed to the hospital. The doctors took one look at the break and realized it was much too severe for them to deal with, so they decided he had to go to Seattle. They trussed him up in a Thompson splint, which was a lightweight steel frame with a turnbuckle, for the trip.

The only transport available in Port Townsend was a hearse, which he was loaded into, and they sped off to the Kingston ferry dock. Skip was jostled around in the back of the hearse, and he mentioned to the funeral home driver that the ride was really rough. The driver came back with, "I wouldn't know, I've never had any complaints from my regular customers." They finally boarded the ferry, where Clarence was in the wheelhouse. Skip made sure that his dad didn't find out he was aboard, let alone laid out in the back of a hearse.

He was taken to the Marine Hospital on Beacon Hill where he remained for a month. He was an outpatient for six months. During his stay, he watched the fire at Todd Shipyards burn below him, as they frantically worked to get the ferry, Kalakala, which was in the drydock, away from the huge blaze. They threw off the lines holding the drydock in place, and tugs towed her out into the bay as she sat high and dry and helpless to save herself.

When Skip was able to go back to work, he spent several months in the office with his leg in a cast. He didn't return to the tugs for seven months, and when he did enter the wheelhouse at the end of March, 1965, he was in a full leg brace. In the next two and a half months he worked fifty-eight days, dragging that leg brace around, on four different boats, the last one being the Prosper.

On one trip with the Phillips Foss, Skip was maneuvering the tug into the locks and the commotion woke the mate. Groggy and not thinking clearly, he walked out on deck and relieved himself over the side of the boat. As he stood there exposed, in the classic man-taking-a-leak pose, he realized where he was, and looked up to see that he had an entranced audience on the lock wall.

In June of 1965, the Seattle Aquarium acquired a killer whale. The aquarium's director, Ted Griffin, purchased the orca from a couple of fishermen in Namu, British Columbia, who had found the whale in their gill nets. Mr. Griffin had a 40' x 60' pen built in the village, of steel mesh supported by oil drums, to transport the whale back to Seattle.

News of the capture was picked up by KVI Radio's DJ, Bob Hardwick, and he hyped the event for all it was worth. Hardwick loved audacious stunts, and he planned to take a little tugboat, the Robert E. Lee, up there and bring back this twenty-two foot, four ton whale. But, it turned out that his boat just didn't have enough horsepower to tow the heavy pen. It had taken the entire village to lift the pen into the water after it was completed.

At this point, Foss Launch and Tug stepped forward and offered their services. So, on July 10, the tugs Iver Foss and Lorna Foss left Seattle for Port Hardy, B.C., at the north end of Vancouver Island. At the helm of the 65' Iver Foss was Captain George Losey, and in command

IVER AND LORNA FOSS AT SEATTLE'S PIER 56, DURING THE WELCOMING CEREMONY FOR THE WHALE, NAMU.

LORNA FOSS WITH WHALE PEN ASTERN.

KOMO-TV CAMERAMEN ON TOP OF LORNA FOSS'S WHEELHOUSE.

IVER FOSS TOWING NAMU.

of the 79' Lorna Foss was Captain Skip Lampman.

At Port Hardy, way up in Queen Charlotte Strait, they put the Iver's towline on the pen and headed south, with Lorna close by. They were accompanied by an entourage of news people, film makers, and the irrepressible Hardwick, who was on board the Robert E. Lee. They made the four hundred mile trip to Seattle at about one and a half to two knots, a typical log towing speed. The Seattle Times and the P.I. were full of news of the journey of the whale Ted Griffen had named Namu, as the reporters filed their daily stories from the tugs. KOMO-TV had their own crew on board the Lorna, providing the Puget Sound area with visual reports.

They had to duck out of the weather from time to time, and they had to contend with tremendous currents in the narrow passages. The durability of the pen was always a concern, although there were people in Seattle who would have loved to see the thing sink, and the whale swim free. The topography of British Columbia presented the two tugboat skippers with their greatest challenges; challenges that many thought were insurmountable in this case.

The huge land mass of Vancouver Island separates the inside water of the B.C. coast from the Pacific Ocean. At either end of the island are entrances to these inside waters. The Strait of Juan de Fuca to the south, ten miles wide and sixty miles long, forms one entrance. The other entrance to the north is Queen Charlotte Sound which is wide open to the Pacific. The Strait of Georgia runs along the lower half of the east coast of Vancouver Island, and the upper region is made up of a complex network of narrow, convoluted passages, inlets, and sounds.

Twice a day, a tremendous volume of water tries to flush in and out as the tide ebbs and flows. At the upper end of the Strait of Georgia, around Quadra Island, the water coming in from each end of Vancouver Island meets. The constriction of the water's flow along the upper half of Vancouver Island results in velocities of up to twenty knots through the narrow channels, accompanied by whirlpools, overfalls, tide rips, and eddies. These whirlpools have sucked large vessels down, never to be seen again. Even the whales in the area wait for slack water before attempting passage of some of these narrows.

Among the most hazardous rapids are the Yacultas, near the entrance to Bute Inlet. These are two rapids over a stretch of four miles in a twisting channel filled with whirlpools and powerful eddies, where there is never slack water. The northernmost island actually gets a bow wave.

Seymour Narrows, about six miles above Campbell River, is a favorite fishing spot for sea birds waiting for torn and maimed fish to boil to the surface of the rapids. The rapids attain a velocity of fifteen knots and are only a third of a mile wide. These narrows loomed large in the skippers' minds. They would have to hit Seymour at exactly slack water, and it would be agonizingly slow going, at a knot and a half, through that mile and a half stretch. However, the procession navigated the narrows at 04:00 A.M. without any problem, as they began the fifth day of the tow.

The tugs cleared customs days later, without having to put into port, because the Customs official flew from Friday Harbor and inspected them while they were under way.

By Sunday, July 25, the skippers were faced with negotiating yet another pass. Sunday afternoon they waited behind Burrows Island for slack tide at Deception Pass. They planned to run down the sheltered east side of Whidbey Island through Skagit Bay and Saratoga Passage, rather than tangle with any sea conditions that might come off the Strait of Juan de Fuca. They were not alone in their wait. Burrows Bay was filled with boats, some nearly colliding in their eagerness to glimpse the whale. At 8:23 P.M. the tugs started through the pass with Namu, and everyone was amazed to see hordes of people lining the bridge railing and covering the surrounding cliffs, yelling and waving to Namu. They went through the pass in the glow of a golden sunset.

Several hours later, a thunderstorm rolled over them, whipping up the shallow waters of Skagit Bay, while lightning flared and crackled spectacularly in the clouds piled overhead. Hardwick kept watch back at the whale pen as they plowed slowly through the night. When the sheltering mass of Whidbey Island slid away astern, the skippers elected to cross over to the western shore of Puget Sound with its potential hiding places from the unstable weather. They had no sooner reached the other side of the sound, when the wind kicked up and they ducked into Appletree Cove at about 6:00 P.M. to wait out the blustery conditions. At 01:00 the next morning the flotilla left its anchorage near the Kingston ferry terminal, and moved around the bulge of President Point into the greater protection of Port Madison. Seattle Seafair representatives on board the Sightseer, came over for a look at Namu, as another electrical storm prowled the area.

After nosing out into Puget Sound several times to test the conditions, and deciding that it was too rough, Captain Losey made the decision to run for Seattle at 11:00 A.M., quartering into a south-southwesterly swell. They pulled into Elliott Bay late in the afternoon of July 26, and took in the tow wire for an overnight wait inside of Duwamish Head.

The next morning they towed Namu's pen to the Seattle waterfront for the frenzied welcoming ceremonies at Pier 56, which were covered by the media nationwide. The tugboat men were applauded for accomplishing a job that had been considered impossible. Both skippers were happy to turn over their controversial cargo, and complete the most bizarre towing assignment of their careers.

In mid-January 1966, Skip was assigned as captain on the Deborah Foss, one of the new 'D' boats. They were all 66' x 24', powered with twin Caterpillar diesels providing 1200 h.p., and all having names starting with D. Deborah had spent the warm months in Alaska, and had come south for service on Puget Sound for the rest of the year.

Skip's first job with the Deborah was to tow an oil barge to the refinery at Anacortes. While waiting for the barge to be loaded, Skip was sitting in the wheelhouse after dinner, listening to the lowband shortwave radio, happy to be tied up in a sheltered harbor. The wind was blowing in excess of sixty knots, a screaming westerly off of the ocean, barreling down the Strait of Juan de Fuca.

As Skip listened to the radio, he heard the tug, George S, call for help. She was en route with Captain Frank Miller, from Seattle to Blubber Bay, at the north end of Texada Island, in B.C., towing an LST barge for American Tow Boat Company. Prior to the trip she had had an engine overhaul on her Fairbanks-Morse diesel. While coming up from Seattle the engine developed problems, and by the time they reached Partridge Bank they knew they were in trouble. They were in an area where westerly storms roll in unimpeded from the Pacific, and smack into Whidbey Island at Point Partridge. They limped along for another five miles as seas pounded them, until they were abeam of Smith Island, a ragged patch of rock with a light on it, where the engine stopped altogether. The barge overtook the boat, putting them in a dangerous situation and they called for help.

Skip got on the radio to the Foss dispatcher in Bellingham and explained the George S's predicament, asking for an okay to go out and give assistance. The dispatcher told him to call the company office in Seattle, and Seattle told him he couldn't go. Someone called Captain Miller on the George S, and told him that Skip was in Anacortes. Frank called Skip to tell him that when they tried to restart the engine with an infusion of kerosene, the tug had shot forward with such velocity that it had broken the tow wire, and they were in a terrible fix.

Skip was very agitated. He had been taught that the rule of the sea is that mariners render aid to any person or vessel in trouble on the water. Skip called Bellingham again, to tell them of the new development, and the company's answer was still "no." He then called the higher-ups in Seattle and implored them to let him go, saying, "these guys are afraid for their lives." The Foss executive said, you're right; we've got to help.

Skip fired up the Deborah and headed out to Rosario Strait. When he was at Burrows Island, Captain Miller called to say they had managed to restart the engine, but that the barge was adrift. The George S was heading for the shelter of nearby James Island before the engine died again. Skip and his crew went after the barge which was bucking and rolling in big beam seas. Fortunately, there was a ladder amidships on the lee side of the barge, and the mate, Darryl Davis, leapt onto the rungs and scrambled up onto the deck of the barge and, using a heaving line, brought the tug's towing bridles up, one by one, to the bitts on the forward end of the barge. Then he threw himself off of the barge, in a well-timed leap, onto the Deborah's wildly plunging aft deck, and they let out the tow wire and brought the barge under control.

Captain Miller brought the George S into the lee of James Island and anchored her in the relative calm. The Deborah towed the barge out of the worst of the weather and stood by until American Tow Boat's tug, Mary D. Hume, arrived and then handed it off to her.

Skip did some interesting jobs with the Deborah. He towed a drydock from Lake Union Drydock to General Construction Company's graving dock on the Duwamish River. To get there, he had to go through three drawbridges on his way to the locks. The drydock was three hundred and eighty feet long and seventy-nine feet wide, making it a tight squeeze through the locks.

The same month, he towed the 504' tanker, Point Loma, through the locks, up the ship canal, through four drawbridges and the two floating bridges, all the way to the south end of Lake Washington, to the Republic Creosote dock at Kennydale.

He even had a run-in with Clarence, who was skipper on the Kalakala. Skip was inbound with an oil barge, coming into Elliott Bay doing eight knots. Clarence was heading for Seattle's Colman Dock. Skip could see that they were converging, but had no way to communicate with Clarence, because there were no radios on the ferries. Skip had passed ahead of the Kalakala near Duwamish Head and was pretty well committed. Clarence made a last-minute course change and went astern of Deborah's barge, narrowly escaping calamity. When Skip and Clarence talked about it later, Clarence said he couldn't believe that tugs could make the kind of speed the Deborah was making.

IVER FOSS, OSWELL FOSS, SEA CHICKEN INSIDE PROTECTION ISLAND, JULY 16, 1956.

DEBORAH FOSS

DEBORAH FOSS TOWING A DRYDOCK FROM LAKE UNION DRYDOCK TO GENERAL CONST. CO's GRAVING DOCK ON THE DUWAMISH RIVER.

DEBORAH AND CAROL FOSS, POINT LOMA. SEATTLE P.I. PHOTO

GAIL MASSOTH

After Clarence un-retired, he skippered many ferries, including the Kalakala.

CHAPTER THIRTEEN

Skip's childhood memories of his father being gone for days on end, as well as his own family obligations, influenced his decision to take the risk of starting his own business so that he could be at home more often. He set himself up in the marine engine repair business. His years of working on old tugboats with cranky machinery, and his experience with many different boat systems and types of equipment had enhanced his natural mechanical aptitude. He also designed and built boathouses, using his years of industrial arts training. He named his enterprise Inlet Marine Towing and Repairs.

In his spare time he was rebuilding, with Clarence, the old tug they had bought together in 1960. When their work on the Elk II was done, they had a beautiful tug with varnished window frames, brass portholes and railings, and oiled wood decks. They hung rubber fenders on her bow and installed a tow winch on her stern. The interior reflected their years of being aboard tugs with few comforts. She had a fine oil burning cook stove, a sink, and icebox, and a fold-up moveable table and seats in a small galley, aft of the engine room. To get to the galley, the crew either went through the engine compartment with its low headroom, or out on deck and in through the aft door. There were berths in the forepeak, and a head with a sink and toilet between the wheelhouse and engine room. The wheelhouse had a padded bench seat, and up behind that was a berth. The wheelhouse had two side doors that could be opened all the way and hooked during warm weather. She wasn't fancy but she was well built.

Skip's son and daughter were all over the boat during the recon-

SETTING THE TOW WINCH IN PLACE ON THE ELK, SKIP ON THE AFT DECK.

THREE GENERATIONS OF LAMPMANS: CLARENCE, SKIP, AND MIKE, JUNE 1967.

struction. These were children descended from two generations of tugboat men on the Lampman side, and the genes of Norwegian fishermen and boatbuilders on the Lillehei side of the family. Having spent their young years playing on Liberty Bay and at their grandparents' Tracyton home on Dyes Inlet, they became boat kids at an early age. Clarence had them in a rowboat when they were tiny, and he invited them into the pilot house with him on the ferries.

Skip's son, Mike could run a tugboat when he was a young boy. One summer the family lashed a cooler onto the back deck, and took off in the Elk II for some cruising in the waters of British Columbia. They moseyed on up through the Canadian Gulf Islands, and then crossed the Strait of Georgia to get to some beautiful cruising spots on the mainland side. The weather and sea conditions were calm and pleasant as they started across, but the wind came up and kicked up a nasty chop. Skip was braced at the wheel, and his wife and daughter were hanging on and turning green, but Mike was belowdecks looking out a porthole as the boat pitched and rolled through the seas. He sang out, "Hey, Dad it's like being in a submarine!" He was having a great time.

As Skip and Clarence were putting the finishing touches on the Elk, Skip was approached by some Poulsbo businessmen who were looking for a boat to take them fishing in Canada. So, at the end of July, five guys showed up with fishing gear and lots of booze for their trip to Campbell River. They took three kicker boats along, and chased fish around for ten days. They had such a good time that they chartered the Elk for years, to go north in search of salmon.

With the Elk operational, Skip began to get an occasional towing job. When he started building boathouses, he would tow the completed boathouse from his beach to its new moorings, using the Elk. Les Baker, Skip's boyhood friend, helped him build the boathouses. They built the first ones right on the beach in front of Skip's house, and when the tide went out they sat cockeyed because of the slope of the ground. Skip had the idea to build them on an old wooden barge he had bought for $500. The barge was patched with plywood on the sides and was a leaky old thing. The plan was to tow the completed boathouse on the barge to Poulsbo, where it was going to be moored, sink the barge, and

ELK II, IN POULSBO, PEPPER ON THE BOW, DOG OF THE WATCH.

ELK II AS SHE LOOKED IN THE '40S. SHE WAS ORIGINALLY POWERED BY A 2 CYL. 36 H.P. CORLISS. SHE WAS OWNED BY JOHN TROXELL FROM 1918, WHEN SHE WAS BUILT, UNTIL 1946.

float the boathouse into place using the Elk.

When the barge was filled with water, it wouldn't sink. Its deck stayed about a foot above the surface of the water. The guys scratched their heads about that for a while, and decided to get some pipes, put them under the boathouse, and roll it to the edge of the barge, and push it off. The idea worked great but, to everyone's surprise, when the boathouse hit the water, the breeze captured it, and it set sail south, down Liberty Bay.

Les was on the barge and Skip was on the Elk, and he took off after it. About the time he caught up with it, the wind would shift, and it would sail off in another direction. As the boathouse skimmed across the bay, Skip chased it back and forth until he managed to get a hold of it and drag it back to where it was supposed to be. Les, from his vantage point on the barge, had a great view of the whole hilarious spectacle.

As Skip's towing business increased, he would take his son, Mike, along when he could, as well as the family dog, an English Setter named Pepper. On trips to Steilacoom, south to Tacoma for gravel, or around to Quilcene on Hood Canal to pick up a barge, to go to Blaine, or Totten Inlet in south sound, Clarence would go along and stand watch.

On one trip the Elk, with Skip at the wheel, was running light to pick up a barge. The deckhand was making pancakes for breakfast. Pepper stuck his head in the galley door, flashing the classic starving dog look at the cook who took pity on him and slipped him a pancake, which Pepper took and disappeared. Pretty soon he was back and the cook gave him another pancake, and off he went. Then he was back again to get another pancake, and this went on for a while.

When they pulled in to pick up the barge, they used a towline that was coiled on the aft deck. They put their towing bridles onto the barge and started moving away, letting out towline. As the line uncoiled, pancakes that Pepper had carefully stashed started flying in all directions.

Several times, Skip was hired to tow the old ferry, Skansonia. In April of 1971, she had been purchased from the Washington Department of Highways by Norm Volotin. In June of 1971, she came into Liberty Bay on the end of the Elk's towline, for repairs, causing some heads to turn and residents to wonder if there was a new ferry route they hadn't heard about. The Elk towed her again in March, 1975, to Seattle, through the locks, up the ship canal, and into Lake Union Drydock for haulout work.

The Lampman family hit some rough seas of their own when ten year old Mike became ill. What doctors initially thought was indigestion turned out to be cancer. While the people who loved him were making heavy weather out of it, Mike was getting on with his life. He was crazy about fishing and could often be found out on the dock in front of the house with a fishing pole in his hand. He was also crazy about baseball, and was enthusiastically involved in Little League.

Mike was having chemotherapy treatment for his aggressive, fast growing cancer, while he was in the sixth grade. His teacher, Ken Maguire, would grab boys by their hair if they were displeasing him. Mike told his dad that he sure hoped Mr. Maguire would grab hold of his hair; wouldn't he be surprised when a clump of it came out in his hand.

Mike was busy with Boy Scouts, and was learning to sail. When he would get home from school, he would often go to the neighbor's house with his latest project in his hands, to get advise on how to use a power tool. And he would go with his dad and Pepper on the tug, and as the days went by, and he grew weaker, he would lie in the berth in the wheelhouse with Pepper, while Skip steered the boat.

Even as the cancer raced through his body in the summer of 1972 Mike was still a menace to fish. While in B.C. with relatives, he caught seventeen fish. He was doing what he loved to do.

Later that summer, Skip got a call from Norm Volotin, who said he had four tickets to Disneyland that he couldn't use, and would Skip please take them. In early August, the family flew to California and played together for the final time, at Disneyland. The tumor in Mike's stomach grew so fast that it was visibly bigger each day.

When they returned home from Disneyland, the next morning, Marilyn, Skip's wife found Mike unconscious. She woke Skip and they rushed Mike to Seattle Children's Hospital. Mike did not regain consciousness in the week he was at the hospital. Skip went back to work and while he was standing by with the Elk as his barge was being off-loaded, Mike died. Marilyn couldn't get a hold of Skip, so she drove south to the job site, just south of the Glacier gravel pit at Steilacoom, at Ketron Island. She found Skip and gave him the terrible news, and they rode back together on the Elk, pulling the barge, which they dropped off at Port Orchard, and took the Elk back to Liberty Bay. There was, after all, no need to rush home.

THE FERRY, SKANSONIA, IN TOW OF THE ELK.

SKIP BUILT BOATHOUSES ON THE BEACH IN FRONT OF HIS HOUSE ON LIBERTY BAY.

CHAPTER FOURTEEN

Inlet Marine's towing work steadily increased to the point where Skip decided it was time to add a bigger tug to the business. In April of 1973, he bought the 60' wooden tug, Mystic. She had been built in 1926 as a Kirsten experimental diesel tug. She worked at Grays Harbor for a decade, and was then transferred to the Columbia River by the Inland Navigation Company. Her engine was replaced with a 1000 h.p. diesel to give her more power for river work. She towed barges on the upper Columbia, and was involved in the building of the Bonneville Dam.

Skip put her right to work towing barges from Port Madison to Steilacoom, and from one end of the sound to the other. General Construction hired Inlet Marine to tow loaded barges from Mats Mats quarry, around the south end of Whidbey Island, and up Saratoga Passage to the south end of the Swinomish Slough, fifty-three miles away. The Mystic would meet the Ruby VI which would have an empty barge or two, and they would trade tows. The Mystic would head back to Mats Mats with the empties and wait for them to be loaded. Then she would head for the slough and meet the Ruby VI somewhere along the way, and they would swap barges again. This went on for several weeks, with the Mystic making trips to Everett periodically to bring in equipment and supplies.

Skip was aware that the Mystic had some planks in her hull that needed to be replaced. He took her out of service and put her up on the ways at Port Orchard Marine Railway, and began removing bad wood. When he and his crew were done, there were no planks left on the starboard side, from her bow to aft of her wheelhouse, to well below her waterline. Dry rot had invaded some of the frames, which had to be cut out and replaced, as well.

Replanking the hull was a painstaking process, each plank having to be shaped to fit perfectly with the one below it. Each piece of wood had to be steamed to allow it to conform to the curve of the hull, and then quickly fastened to the frames before the wood cooled and lost its flexibility. Skip was no stranger to shipwright work, so he tackled the job, and the Mystic was soon out on the water again.

Clarence, at the age of eighty-one continued to make many trips on the tugs with Skip, as did Pepper, the dog of the watch.

Pepper was no longer the family's only dog. A young female English Setter named Misty had joined the household. She was aboard the Mystic one day when the cook set a pumpkin pie on the galley table. The top step of the engine room ladder served as a seat for the table. When Misty climbed onto this step her head was even with the tabletop. The crew was busy elsewhere, so Misty was undisturbed as she ate the filling out of the pie, until all that remained as a carefully cleaned crust. It's the only time she ever touched anything on that table.

The ladder down to the engine room was steep, and flanked on one side by a 1271 GM diesel engine, and on the other side by a 271 auxiliary engine. If Skip was working in the engine room, Misty would come down and join him. It didn't matter to her if the rackety auxiliary was running, or the air compressor was noisily cycling on and off. One day Skip was working on something that required him to lie down to get to it. There were several guys in the galley, where they could watch Skip working below, as they drank his coffee and offered advice. Misty climbed down the engine room ladder and plopped down on top of him and made herself comfortable. That, of course, cracked everybody up.

Inlet Marine Towing was hired by Manson Construction and Engineering Company when they began preparing for the construction of Pier 20 on the east side of Seattle's Harbor Island. The land had been contaminated by the Shell Oil plant that had previously been on the site. Manson dug up the polluted soil and dumped it into barges for removal.

The Mystic moving barges.

Replanking the Mystic's hull, Skip on the right.

EMPTY BARGES IN EBEY SLOUGH, WAITING FOR A TOW BACK TO SEATTLE.

It was then taken to Ebey Slough, north of Everett, to a garbage dump on Indian land used by the city of Seattle for years. Manson's A-frame tug, Elmer M, would take the loaded barges from the Pier 20 site and head north with them. Skip, coming from the north in the Mystic with empty barges would meet the Elmer M somewhere on the way, one time as far south as West Point, and swap, taking the loaded barges, three, often four at a time, the rest of the way to Ebey Slough, where they would be unloaded onto the garbage pit, the idea being to cover the pit, which was full.

CHAPTER FIFTEEN

In 1977 Skip had a shot at a big job but he knew the Mystic was not enough boat for the challenges that the job presented.

The natural breakwater at Port Angeles, called Ediz Hook, was being destroyed by the harsh sea conditions of the Strait of Juan De Fuca. It had been estimated that 750,000 tons of rock would be needed to reinforce the narrow two and a half mile long strip of land that jutted into the Strait. Two tugboat outfits had already attempted the job and had encountered overwhelming difficulties.

Skip's search for a larger boat took him to Seattle, where he found a tug that was 92', and he just had a good feeling about her. She had been built of steel in 1923 by the Craig Shipbuilding Company of Long Beach, California, as the diesel tug, John F. Craig. She was sold to Haviside Marine, of San Francisco, and worked for many years as the H.T. Haviside. She had later been sold to Murphy Pacific Marine Salvage Company, of San Francisco, and her name changed to Ellen Murphy. Skip bought her from Morton Marine Company, of Seattle. He named her the Magic. She was, at the time, the second largest independent tugboat on Puget Sound.

He began the Port Angeles job in December, making twenty to twenty-one trips a month, taking tandem (2) General Construction barges, each with a 2500 ton load of rock from Mats Mats to Port Angeles, forty miles away. In good weather the trip took fourteen hours. In stormy weather it could take up to eighteen hours. They made a round trip every twenty-four hours, taking the empty barges back, after putting the loaded ones in the slip, coming in with them on the tow wire;

THE TUG, H.T. HAYISIDE IN SAN FRANCISCO, 1946.
NATIONAL MARITIME MUSEUM, S.F., PHOTO.

MISTY ON THE BOW OF THE ELLEN MURPHY, WITH SKIP, THE DAY HE TOOK DELIVERY OF HER.

THE MAGIC WITH THE ZAG BARGE AT BANGOR.

a move that became so practiced that they had the barges tied up in fifteen minutes and were on their way to pick up the empties.

One trip from Mats Mats took twenty-two hours. From the quarry to Port Townsend was only nine miles, but on that day they were battered by seventy knot winds, with seas crashing over the bow and the Magic's decks awash, so they turned into Port Townsend to wait out the storm. A few hours later, when the wind had subsided to forty knots, the Magic plunged back out into the heaving seas. When they straggled into Port Angeles twenty-two hours later, they found that 300 tons of rock had been washed overboard.

The job lasted about a year and a half, during which time they hauled 876,000 tons of rock. Skip's gamble to buy the Magic had paid off.

Skip had a change in canine companions when he purchased the Magic. Up to that time, Pepper had been dog of the watch, faithfully accompanying Skip on all of his tugboat trips. Pepper took an instant dislike to the Magic, and was extremely reluctant to go with Skip a second time. The Union diesel would make a loud backfire noise when it started up and Pepper, who was terrified of loud bangs, would have nothing to do with it. Misty, on the other hand, unfazed by noise, liked the boat. As Skip rowed the resisting Pepper out to the Magic, Misty came swimming after them. Skip dragged her on board and a tacit agreement was reached that Pepper would stay home and Misty would be the new boat dog.

The crew of the Magic had a rope ring they would use to try to make rope ringers from the boat deck, down to the bow winch on the main deck. Misty would retrieve the ring and run up the steep ladder with it. Someone would throw it and Misty would scramble back down the ladder to fetch it. As long as somebody tossed it, she would go get it; even when she was heavily pregnant, which she was seven months into the Port Angeles job. When she would get sleepy, she would curl up for a snooze in Skip's room behind the wheelhouse.

She gave birth to eight puppies, but wasn't too interested in them. Pepper was quite taken with them, though. He was sweet and patient with them, which was unusual for a male dog. He would stay with them for hours at a time. One day Skip's wife left the house to run some errands, and the puppies managed to get out of their outside enclosure. Pepper coaxed all eight puppies into a part of the yard that penned them in, and he sat on a low embankment to watch them. When a puppy would crawl up the bank, he would nudge it with his nose and it would tumble back down into the yard. He did this until someone came home to relieve him of the job.

He would romp with the puppies until they were worn out. He would wait until they were all asleep, and if one was still playful he would knock it over with his nose until it closed its eyes in exhaustion. Then he would streak out of the yard and go cruise the neighborhood.

The Magic did not sit idle in the months before the Port Angeles job began. She and the Mystic had towed barges from Everett to Indian Island. Guy F. Atkinson Construction built an ammunition pier for the Navy facility, and Skip's boats towed loads of concrete pilings to the site, as well as tending Atkinson's pile driver, Mr. Guy.

In January 1979, Inlet Marine landed another big job, made possible because of the Magic. Construction was underway on a Trident submarine facility at the Naval Submarine Base at Bangor. A massive structure called the Delta Pier projected out into Hood Canal which, when finished, would service submarines. The first Trident sub was expected to arrive in November of 1981.

The Magic was hired to bring in concrete aggregate for Hoffman Construction Company. Skip leased an innovative self-unloading barge called the ZAG 501 for the project. This 250' x 63' x 16' barge had a 100' conveyor belt to discharge its 4800 ton load at 1000 tons per hour.

The location of the job site made it necessary to have the Hood Canal Bridge opened every time they came through. As though to eliminate this obstacle, in February a storm blew in packing winds of such ferocity that they destroyed one end of the bridge, sinking the floating span, making Skip's work over the next two years much easier.

The huge pier required a tremendous amount of concrete. Skip, with Magic and the ZAG, brought in two 4800 ton loads of three different materials a week from Steilacoom, to total 885,000 tons of aggregate to the job site.

In January of 1980, Clarence and Skip said their final good-byes. Clarence, ever the bigger-than-life presence in his son's life, passed on.

Elsie had died in 1976 when Clarence had gotten them into an automobile wreck; a devastating event for Clarence. Skip, only halfway through the Trident job, had many hours alone in the wheelhouse on the one hundred and thirty mile round trip to mourn his dad's passing, and remember their times together.

The Magic and the Mystic teamed up for a job in Bellingham, the construction of the Louisiana-Pacific settling basin. The Magic, with Skip at the wheel, towed General Construction barges to Victoria, B.C., to get the material used in the basin, sandwiched between her two trips a week with the ZAG to Trident. The Mystic tended the dredges and towed the loaded dump scow into Bellingham Bay and dumped it. She also ran to Tacoma to bring barge loads of pipe to the Bellingham job site.

The Mystic's skipper was afraid to go around the outside of Whidbey Island from Bellingham, choosing instead to go through the Swinomish Slough with the empty barge. The narrowness of the slough requires that it be navigated precisely, especially with a barge, because there is little margin for error. The town of LaConner, with its docks and marina tightens up the channel even more, and the current running through there can make things tricky. At its southern end, the slough makes a bend along a high rock wall, and culminates in a mile-long passage through mud flats by way of an extremely skinny channel. To either side of this channel is log storage.

The skipper misjudged the channel and put the Mystic into the shallows, where she sucked up mud through her cooling water intake. When the engine began to run hot, he did not clean out the strainer or attempt to do anything about the problem. The Mystic made it to Tacoma and picked up her load. On the trip back to Bellingham, the engine continued to run hot.

The skipper, now afraid to make another pass through the slough, decided to go to the west of Whidbey Island. As the tug approached Point Partridge, the engine alarm went off when the engine overheated. The skipper silenced the alarm and continued on north. At Point

MISTY PEERING ANXIOUSLY FROM THE BOW.

MISTY COMING DOWN THE MAGIC'S LADDER. THE MAGIC UNDERWAY WITH A BARGE ALONGSIDE.

Partridge the engine seized up. The sea conditions were sloppy; uncomfortable, but not bad. With the boat dead in the water, the skipper called the office and told them the problem. Skip's wife then called him on the Magic, which was at Bangor. He said to tell him I'm on my way, tell him not to do anything, I'll be there in an hour and a half.

Mystic's skipper disregarded Skip's instructions and called the Coast Guard. He had failed to mention that the tug had collided with the rake of the barge when they were in Bellingham, and had stove in the hatch combing so that it would not close. As a result, some water was slopping into the boat and the crew panicked. They did not use the gas powered scow pump to clear the bilge. When the Coast Guard arrived by helicopter, they lifted off the skipper, who couldn't swim. The Coast Guard instructed the crew to cut the barge loose.

The Coast Guard put a line on the Mystic to tow her, without checking the tug's rudder position. They began towing her with the rudder hard over. The moment they began to pull on her bow, she sheered off to one side, rolled over and sank within forty-five seconds. The Coast Guard fished the crew out of the water and left the scene.

When Skip arrived, all he could find was the barge on the beach. The weather was too rough to salvage the barge for several days, and Skip had to keep up on the Bangor run. Al Lieske finally managed to get a hold of the barge and pulled it off of the beach with the tug, Thelma S. Most of the bottom ripped out of it, so that it was floating on the tops of the internal tanks in the hull. The damage to the barge was many thousands of dollars. Skip actually kept the Mystic's skipper on the payroll.

Skip loved the Mystic's wonderful maneuverability. She handled beautifully and was very responsive. He could put a line on the barge to her bow and she could zigzag backwards down the bay. Skip mourned the loss of this fine tug.

Skip was in immediate need of a tug to replace the Mystic. He could not meet his commitments with just the Magic, so he began searching for another boat.

He found a steel tug named the Cowlitz that had been owned by Shaver Transportation Company of Portland, Oregon, for many years.

Shaver's tugs ran from Astoria to the Dalles on the Columbia River, and up the Willamette River, through Portland, as far as Newberg. They did ship towing and assists, log towing, and barging of bulk commodities such as grain and petroleum products.

The Cowlitz had been named the Wilavis, but in 1947, Shaver renamed six of their tugs after local rivers, the Cowlitz being one of them. She had worked on the Cowlitz River, which winds between Kelso and Longview, as an icebreaker, among her other duties. Knappton Towboat Company of Portland bought her in the seventies and she continued to do the same type of towing in the same area.

Skip went down to Portland to take a look at her. She had been built in 1929 at Portland. She was 66' x 16' x 8', and was powered by a 750 h.p. Fairbanks-Morse diesel, which had been installed in 1964. Skip bought her and ran her up the coast to Seattle in May of 1979, and named her the Mystery. He put her to work towing the ZAG from Steilacoom to Bangor, and she finished that job, freeing up the Magic to do other things.

The Magic's old Union diesel, though very handsome with its shiny brass fittings, was not putting out the 560 horsepower it should have been. Several modifications to the engine and the propellor by previous owners had taken their toll. When Skip towed the ZAG with the Mystery on the Bangor job, she made much better time than the Magic, even though she was smaller. It was time to repower the Magic.

One of Skip's friends heard about a pair of Fairbanks-Morse, 1600 h.p., 10 cylinder opposed piston engines in Tacoma, that had come out of the decommissioned destroyer escort, Cannonade, and before that had been in a submarine. (On the subs, they had four of these engines, three on line, and one being overhauled at all times.) With two engines, Skip could install one in the Magic, and use the other one for parts as repairs became necessary. The engines were available, affordable, and would fit in the Magic, so Inlet Marine bought them.

To get the big thirty-two ton Union out of the boat, Skip had to cut out the entire boat deck aft of the wheelhouse, including the stack, as well as the aft bulkhead of the house on the main deck. The Union was lifted out with a crane at the Manson Construction yard, thanks to the

THE COWLITZ IN OREGON, THE DAY SKIP STARTED BACK TO SEATTLE WITH HER, MAY 1979.

MYSTERY JUGGLING THE BARGE PERMANENTE 27, ON THE DUWAMISH RIVER AT THE GLACIER SAND AND GRAVEL PLANT.

generosity of Hawk Edwards, a founding father at Manson.

The Magic was then towed to Tacoma by Al Lieske's tug, Thelma S, and the Fairbanks which had its engine bed attached was lowered into the yawning hole in the Magic. Everything would have to be arranged to fit the new engine. Pipes for oil and cooling water had to be removed and new piping and heat exchangers installed.

Skip's mate during this repower was Jerry Jensen. He was a great guy, willing to work hard and accept directions without his ego getting all twisted out of shape. He always put forth his best effort in a pleasant manner.

With the Magic opened up like a tin can, it was cold in the engine room in the winter. They had rigged up a tarp over the opening to keep the moisture out. One morning Skip came down to the Magic after a night of snowfall. He had not seen Jerry pull up some of the diamond plate steel deck plates the night before, and set them on edge.

It was very dark in the engine room as Skip climbed down the ladder. As he stepped off of the last rung, expecting the deck to be under his feet, he plunged straight into the bilge. His flailing arms brought one of the heavy deck plates down onto his head. He could have been seriously injured, but he didn't break any bones, just had some nasty bumps and bruises. When Jerry arrived and found out what had happened, he was horrified. Comments about Skip's thick Norwegian head passed among the crew.

When the installation was finished, the Magic rode a foot higher out of the water because the Fairbanks weighed sixteen tons less than the Union. The repower took almost six months.

As Skip's towing business continued to grow, in 1980 he decided to make it a separate entity from Inlet Marine, naming it Inlet Towing, Inc.

Skip had negotiated a contract with Glacier Sand and Gravel Company, in 1979, to supply their Duwamish and Tacoma plants, towing loaded barges from the gravel pit at Steilacoom. The contract was renewed in 1982, keeping the Magic and Mystery busy. As short-term towing jobs would require the diversion of one of his boats, he would have to

THE FAIRBANKS-MORSE, 10 CYLINDER, OPPOSED PISTON ENGINE.

REPOWERING THE MAGIC. HER STACK, BOAT DECK, AND AFT BULKHEAD WERE CUT OUT TO ALLOW ACCESS TO THE ENGINE ROOM.

MYSTERY TOWING A MANSON DERRICK BARGE ON THE DUWAMISH RIVER.

THE ZAG BARGE OFFLOADING GRAVEL FOR FILL BETWEEN PIERS 90 & 91 ON THE NORTH END OF SEATTLE'S ELLIOTT BAY.

hire other tugs occasionally to meet the Glacier towing schedule.

Skip's company landed a nice towing contract in 1981, as part of the West Seattle Bridge construction. The Mystery towed the ZAG, bringing in concrete aggregate for the huge structure, as well as fill material from the Steilacoom pit.

In October, 1983, Inlet Towing added another tug to its fleet; the 55' 800 h.p. Goblin. Skip immediately put her to work on a five month job towing from Steilacoom to the Glacier Hylebos plant in Tacoma, in addition to the regular gravel runs.

With the two smaller tugs taking care of the contract work, Inlet Towing was able to bid jobs where they could use the Magic and the ZAG barge. One of these jobs was the I-90 Bridge expansion in the mid-1980s. The Magic towed material from Steilacoom to Pier 20 on the east side of Harbor Island, where it was off-loaded and trucked to the I-90 westbound embankment job site on Lake Washington.

Another project involved the Magic and the ZAG towing fill material to Pier 90-91, below the Magnolia Bridge. The area between the two piers was filled with 250,000 tons of gravel brought in from Steilacoom, to make an automobile storage facility for ships bringing in cars.

Towing to Steilacoom could be boring, taking the same route day after day, but there were moments of excitement every once in a while. One such moment occurred on a run back from Steilacoom without a barge. It was the mate's watch, and Skip had gone to bed. They were just seven and a half miles into the trip, about a mile beyond the Narrows Bridge when the mate fell asleep at the helm, and the Magic ran full bore up onto Salmon Beach on the Tacoma side of the narrows, throwing Skip out of his bunk. When he picked himself up off of the deck and ran to see what the hell had happened, the Magic's bow was just a few feet from someone's yard. Skip checked to make sure that the Magic wasn't holed, and backed her off the beach, causing quite a racket with revving engine and prop wash. She had to be drydocked for extensive, and expensive, repairs.

Skip made a trip to Blaine with the Magic for Manson Construction,

Skip & Misty on the Goblin, crew member setting up a barge lantern.

The Goblin with a barge at Mats Mats Quarry.

The Mystery with the Zag, in Elliott Bay. Skip sold the boat, but it didn't work out, which is why she has a different company name on her, April 1989.

towing their big derrick barge, Wotan. He dropped off the barge and headed back in the afternoon, running light for Seattle. They had no sooner started back when a heavy fog developed. They fired up the radar, only to discover that there was no output to the radar screen; it was blank, and they were blind. So they did it the old fashioned way, they navigated their way through the San Juans blowing the whistle and using echoes from the shore, steering by compass, never seeing land as they slowly made their way south along the eastern shoreline of Puget Sound. As they came into the approach to the locks, they found they were fifty feet from where they thought they were. The Shilshole Marina breakwater suddenly loomed up right in front of them, and the Magic's bow dug into a little sandy area on the jetty, just feet from the channel. It was the first thing they had seen since leaving Blaine.

In the mid-eighties, Skip lost his companion of many years, Misty. She had been a fine, faithful friend over the many miles she and Skip traveled together. When his grief had subsided, he felt the need to fill the void left by Misty's passing. He soon began looking for another English Setter. He found a feisty little one year old female to whom he gave the name, Cap's Dusty Doll, and generally referred to her as Dusty, unless he was feeling especially affectionate, and then it was Doodle.

Shortly after Skip brought her home, he took her to work. She had been born and raised in a kennel environment, so this was strange, new territory for her.

The Magic was tied to the outside of the ZAG barge, and they had to cross the deck of the barge, with all of its machinery, to get to the boat. Dusty stayed close to Skip, following his every move until she strayed too close to the side of the barge and fell overboard. Skip hauled her out of the water, and she never fell off of a barge again. From then on, when the ZAG was unloading, Dusty would be right at Skip's side, in the midst of clanking machinery and moving conveyor belts.

Skip was always doing maintenance on the boats, keeping everything running and looking shipshape. As he concentrated on the job at hand, his tools began to disappear. A wire brush, a piece of sandpaper that he had just used, would vanish. He thought that maybe he was losing his marbles. Then, on the Magic he would go to his room behind the wheelhouse to clean up, and the sink stopper would be missing. He would replace the stopper, and pretty soon he wouldn't be able to find it.

He was rooting around in his room one day, looking for something, when he found a pile of tools and odds and ends that he had been looking all over for. Dusty was furtively picking them up and surreptitiously making off with them, stashing them near her bed in Skip's room. As the sink stoppers continued to disappear, the only thing he could figure was that she was eating them, so he made it a habit to put the rubber plug up on a shelf, out of Dusty's reach, when he wasn't using it.

The Magic had no inside access to the wheelhouse; the crew had to go out on deck and up a ladder to get there. When the weather was really rough and waves were flying over the bulwarks, anyone wanting to get to the wheelhouse had to go aft, climb onto the tow winch, pull themselves up onto the boat deck, go forward and duck quickly into a door. This arrangement could be bothersome because there was no head on the upper deck. There was an intercom that facilitated communications between decks.

One early January day, Skip was running the Magic with Myron, the mate. The weather had been crummy for some time and Skip had a feeling it was going to get worse. He called down to Myron, and told him to close the aft engine room door. Myron went out the galley door and put it on the hook so that it was partially open. Then he went aft to secure the engine room door. While he was doing that, Dusty who had been cooped up inside, jumped out on deck to relieve herself. Myron came back to the galley and closed the door.

The Magic was soon taking water over her decks. Some time later, Skip called down to ask Myron if he had seen Dusty. Myron said no, she must be up there with you someplace. Alarmed, Skip left the wheelhouse and climbed down the tow winch, and there was Dusty on the aft deck, knee deep in sea water, her rump pressed against the engine room door. If she had been anywhere else on the deck she would have been washed over the side. Skip picked up the cold, terrified dog and took her topside to the wheelhouse for warmth and reassurance.

In the late 1980s, on a trip to Southeastern Alaska with the Magic, Skip was towing two barges in what is called a tandem tow. The barges, loaded with containers full of supplies, were going to the village of Metlakatla for Sig Hale Construction Company.

They were in northern British Columbia headed northwest, up Grenville Channel. The land on each side of the channel rises one thousand to twenty-seven hundred feet, in a sharp V. The channel is forty-five miles long and two tenths of a mile wide in the middle, and at its deepest point is twelve hundred feet deep. The land is covered in dense forest down to the water's edge, and there are waterfalls along the way.

This particular night was rainy and foul on the mate's midnight to six A.M. watch. Traffic was sparse through Grenville, but the mate caught a blip on the radar, indicating that a vessel was coming toward them. It wasn't long before he saw a Canadian tug go by. He looked back through the rain to watch the tug's lights, but they had disappeared, and there was no evidence of the boat on radar. The mate thought that this was so strange that he woke Skip, in his cabin directly behind the wheelhouse.

The mate explained the odd circumstances to Skip who turned on the searchlight and looked back along the 1600' of tow wire with his binoculars. He saw the tug tied to the barge, and he glimpsed men clambering over the equipment lashed to the barge's deck.

Skip turned the Magic around and headed full tilt along the towline to the barge; probably the last thing that tugboat crew would have expected. The men scrambled back aboard the tug and tore off in the opposite direction. They had obscured the name of the boat by draping canvas over it, or painting it out, but the company colors and insignia showed up well in the searchlight's beam.

In May of 1988, Inlet Towing was again hired by Sig Hale Construction Company to take a loaded barge to Ketchikan with the Magic.

Having just cleared the northern end of Vancouver Island, Skip was working his way along the mainland shore. By staying east, the seas rolling in from the Pacific could be taken on the port bow, which was more comfortable than wallowing in beam seas.

The Magic was approaching Cape Caution and a fifteen mile stretch of open ocean, before gaining the protection of Cape Calvert's lee shore. The weather deteriorated rapidly, with the winds rising sharply and veering to northwest. They were moving parallel to the coast line about two miles out, when the towline parted. They had to quickly bring the remaining wire in, and then chase after the barge. When they reached the barge, they were able to get a hold of a heavy line attached to a bitt on the barge, with a pikepole, and make it fast to the stern of the Magic. With that tenuous hold on one corner of the barge, they headed for shelter, which was about three miles distant, northeast in Slingsby Channel. Slingsby Channel is not a place that a tugboat skipper would take a barge, unless he was out of options. There was some very intent chart studying going on in the Magic's pilot house.

Off of the entrance to Slingsby Channel, Skip turned the Magic and the barge, which was being dragged behind them stern first and behaving erratically, and headed for the opening, putting them in beam seas. The tug and barge took some big rolls as they struggled toward the channel, the wind howling at eighty knots. Waves crashed all along the rocky shoreline, even across the channel, the white water making it difficult to find the entrance.

Just inside the channel was Vigilance Cove which they quickly determined would provide no protection at all as waves swept in unimpeded over low rocks. Skip steered the Magic deeper into the channel as the storm intensified. Three quarters of a mile into the channel, it narrows from six hundred yards down to two hundred yards at the Outer Narrows. The British Columbia Pilot says, "with the wind blowing in, the seas break across the entrance, and in the narrowest part, even during calms, the water is much agitated." It further states, "...enter Slingsby Channel from the westward through the outer narrows in fine weather at or near slack water..."

Moving farther along the channel, they found a small bay on the north side of the east end of the channel that was relatively quiet, where Skip opted to wait out the storm. They anchored the tug and barge by catching a pinnacle of rock that rose to within several feet of the surface, with a surge chain they had rigged up between the barge and the boat. From this indentation in the rocks, they were able to see the rapids that form the other end of the five mile channel.

Inland of Slingsby Channel are long inlets and sounds, and at each tide change that huge volume of water tries to rush through the slender opening. At the eastern end of Slingsby are Nakwakto Rapids, through which all of that water flows.

The B.C. Pilot says the rapids are, "400 yards wide, but in the center of the rapids is Turret Island, 80' high against which the tidal current rushed with great fury … The flood current in the rapids commences 3 ½ hours before high water by the shore in Slingsby Channel, and runs with a velocity at springs of 10 to 15 knots…until it is high water at Seymour Inlet; after an interval of 10 minutes slack water the ebb commences and runs…attended by very heavy and dangerous overfalls and attaining a velocity at springs of 20 knots." Slingsby Channel was not a restful anchorage.

As Skip and the crew waited out the storm, Skip saw a Canadian surf boat come charging up the channel toward the rapids, which were running at full ebb. The boat was doing twenty knots and as it hit the rapids it seemed to stop, then it dropped down, and finally jolted upward, slowly bucking the twenty-three knot current.

The B.C. Pilot warns, "If it is necessary to proceed through Nakwakto Rapids, the turn of the stream should be most carefully watched, so that the vessel may with certainty make the passage during the only 10 minutes of slack water, for at no other time would it be possible to do it with any degree of safety."

"These narrows, however, should only be used by a vessel on emergency and after acquiring some practical knowledge by passing through at slack water in a boat. It is also imperative that the tides should be previously watched from Treadwell Bay."

SEEKING SHELTER FROM HIGH WINDS NEAR CAPE CAUTION, B.C.

By 1988, it was common knowledge that the pit at Steilacoom would be running out of gravel in just a few years, so Skip began to scout around for a new source of material. He found a quarry that produced a good quality gravel in British Columbia. The drawback was that the trips were much longer; Steilacoom had been so convenient.

Inlet Towing bid on the Pier 2 and 3 job for the Port of Tacoma, to bring in British Columbia gravel, using the Magic and the ZAG 501 barge. The economic feasibility of transporting gravel such distances was underscored when Skip won the towing contract.

On one trip in January, the Magic was headed north to Jervis Inlet, where the Canadian gravel pit was located. A fierce westerly wind was raising havoc in Puget Sound and the Strait of Juan de Fuca. Off of Point No Point it was very rough, and by the time they clawed their way as far as Port Townsend, the weather was so extreme that they had to take shelter in the bay. On the VHF radio Skip heard a 9000 h.p. Red Stack tug at Point Partridge say he was having to turn back.

By 02:00 A.M., the wind had died down to dead calm so they resumed their trip north. In the Strait of Georgia, off of the mouth of the Fraser River, at a place called Sand Heads, it started to rain. By the time they had gone another forty miles north to Merry Island, it was snowing. Skip's usual shortcut through narrow, winding Agamemnon Channel was so obscured by heavy snowfall that they had to continue north another nine miles to the entrance of Jervis Inlet.

As they turned east up Jervis Inlet, they were buffeted by winds out of Hotham Sound, and the Magic began to ice up. Two hours later they reached the quarry and tied up to the loading dock. About five hundred tons had been loaded when the gravel started to stick to the pit's conveyor belt that delivered the material to the barge. That brought a halt to the loading. All they could do was wait. The temperature continued its plunge and everything at the pit froze.

The pit's crew, who lived there during the week and went home on weekends, had no reason to stay without work to do. There were no roads around the pit, and the crew was transported in and out by small boat. The waters of the inlet were much too rough for the little crew boat, so Skip fired up the Magic and ferried the men to a dock in Agamemnon Bay, six miles away.

For three days the men aboard the Magic were caught in the outflow; wind rushing down the long inlet from the cold, mountainous interior. This outflow condition can generate winds up to one hundred m.p.h. It blew a steady fifty to sixty knots and the temperature remained at 6 degrees Fahrenheit. Every heater in the boat was on full blast, but Skip's room had ice on the inside of the windows. It was so rough at the pit that they ran the tug across the inlet to Goliath Bay three miles away, to get out of the full force of the wind.

Days later, it warmed up just enough to complete the loading of the barge. The trip back to Tacoma was bitingly cold, so that when they arrived, the gravel was a huge, frozen lump. To get the material to thaw, they lit smudge pots and set them under the hoppers full of gravel. As Skip was lighting one of the pots, it tipped over and spilled burning fuel down his front, setting his clothing on fire. He had on heavy gloves and pounded out the flames.

Skip had a skin cancer by his nose that he had consulted a doctor about, and was scheduled to have it removed. The fire scorched his face, burning off the cancer. When he went back to the doctor and told her the story, she said, "Wouldn't it be easier to just let me burn it off? Next time, let me take it off, okay?"

Skip was happy with the material from the Jervis Inlet pit, and put the word out that this product was available. One company that expressed interest was Lakeside Industries. They hired Inlet Towing to supply their Seattle plant, which was on the ship canal. This developed into a long-term business relationship.

Skip started a year-long project with Manson Construction and Engineering Company in 1990, at the north end of Elliott Bay, where a big, new marina was being built.

In July, midway through the project, the Magic broke her Lufkin reduction gear, a costly piece of machinery to replace. The Mystery took over the Elliott Bay Marina towing, as well as the trips to Jervis Inlet for Lakeside and Ash Grove Cement.

Skip needed to charter a boat until he had the time to make the repairs to the Magic. He had to have a tugboat large enough to handle the 250' ZAG on the trips to Jervis Inlet, and he had to have it immediately. He went to Crowley Maritime to see about using one of their laid-up tugs. He looked over the 105' George S, and figured she would be a good boat for the job.

Crowley agreed to lease the tug on a monthly basis. When he signed the lease, they said, oh by the way, she needs some major engine work to get her running. Skip set to work and had her fired up and ready to go in twenty-four hours. The Red Stack people were amazed, having been told by their mechanics that the boat required about $50,000 worth of work to get her going.

This boat was the very same George S that Skip had assisted almost twenty-five years before with the Deborah Foss. Perhaps the George S was demonstrating the law of Karma, that what goes around comes around. At any rate she came out of retirement and went to work for Skip. When it came time for Skip to make the third lease payment, Crowley told him that the George S was too valuable a boat for them to be leasing, and they wanted her returned immediately.

With the George S pulled out from under him, Skip again found himself having to scramble to find a replacement boat. He contacted Marine Leasing and found the Nuka Bay, which he used for the next four months through the completion of the Elliott Bay Marina towing job.

THE GEORGE S AT JERVIS INLET, B.C., WITH THE ZAG. JULY 1990.

THE ZAG 501 BARGE.

CHAPTER SIXTEEN

The cook/deckhand working for Skip in August, 1992, left without warning, leaving Skip short on crew for a trip to Jervis Inlet. He asked me if I would like to come along and cook for one trip. I hadn't cruised to Jervis in ten years and I remembered how beautiful British Columbia was, so I said yes. I had also longed to take a ride on a tugboat and this looked like my chance.

When I signed on for the trip I knew that Skip had been a tugboat skipper for quite a while, but had I realized the extent of his experience, I would have been a little less antsy about the adventure. When I came on board, Skip had over fifty trips to Alaska in his logbook, which meant he had been through British Columbia's Inside Passage at least one hundred times. He had been into Vancouver Harbor over fifty times, including five trips on into Port Moody. He had been up the Fraser River over twenty times. Then there was his extensive, intimate knowledge of Puget Sound waters, the San Juan and Gulf Islands. But I was unaware of all of this water that had passed under his keel as I clambered aboard the Magic.

The crew call out was at 10:00 A.M. Skip had arrived earlier and had the Magic's engine warmed up. For someone not used to loud engines, the roar was unnerving. Skip and the mate brought in the Magic's mooring lines and coiled them on deck. Skip bounded effortlessly up the steep ladder at the forward end of the house, and went into the wheelhouse. He maneuvered the tug around to the barge, turning, reversing, and going forward until the tires on the Magic's starboard side kissed the slab side of the barge. The power of the boat and the bold sure way that

Skip handled her just about took my feet out from under me. The mate, Brian Farsey, climbed from the boat to the barge and began preparing for departure. Lines from the beach to the barge had to be set up for our return, so that the crew could pick them up off of the embankment with pikepoles to secure the barge when it came back loaded.

I knew my way around a boat, having raced sailboats and cruised in power boats, but I was in no way prepared for the scale of everything. The engine was taller than I was, the mooring lines and working lines were so heavy they had to be dragged along the deck. Securing a line to a bitt or a cleat required two hands. Throwing a line for any distance was out of the question.

Skip moved the Magic to the bow of the barge, which loomed above the tug's aft deck. Brian was there, ready to take the port towing bridle, which I handed up to him, and he grabbed it using his pikepole and put it over the port bitt on the barge. Then I handed him the other bridle and he began to walk with it to the starboard side of the barge. Because the nearby shoreline was crowded with other vessels, the barge had to be pulled out from the beach at an angle to clear the obstructions. The Magic was not able to get in close to shore, which meant that the brake on the tow winch had to be released to allow just enough towline out so that the mate could reach the other bitt and drop the eye of the bridle over it. Because we had to navigate the ship canal, bridges, and the locks, the tow wire had to be as short as possible so that Skip would have control of the barge in the confined space. The ship canal is lined with boats and marinas stuffed into every foot along both shores.

Skip watched to make sure that the bridles and the winch brake were secure and then walked forward to the wheelhouse. He gave the Magic some throttle and the barge started moving out of its slot. Skip worked it out into the channel, sliding just feet from a barge tied to the beach. The tow wire moved from side to side as the Magic towed the 180' barge up the canal. We started through the Ballard Bridge, which looked impossibly narrow with that steel box straining at the towing bridles like a restless beast.

As we approached the locks, Skip slowed the Magic to dead slow, just keeping enough way on to keep the barge in line. Looking out the wheelhouse windows, Skip seemed as relaxed as he would be if he were sitting in his living room. This is what he had been doing for thirty-four years, and he handled the tug and barge with easy confidence. The gates to the large locks swung open and the boats locking through from Puget Sound went by us as we waited for the lock chamber to empty of traffic. When the light at the lock entrance turned green, Skip opened up the throttle a bit and the Magic slid slowly down the long chamber to the set of gates at the salt water end. Bryan. who had ridden the barge on the one and a half mile trip, sent a line to the lock attendant, who dropped the eye over a bollard on the lock wall. The mate put the heavy line around the barge's stern bitt, and put another turn on it so that it could slip, but as the forward momentum of the barge lessened, he began to snug it down until the line took the strain and the barge stopped. As the water level dropped in the chamber, he let the line slip just enough to match the rate of descent without allowing the barge to move away from the wall.

The lock gates opened and Skip walked back to the aft controls on the boat deck. With a nod from Skip, the lock attendant dropped the barge's line down to the mate who secured it to the barge so that it wouldn't wash overboard.

He made his way as quickly as he could to the bow of the barge, where I waited with a ladder to get him back aboard the tug. He climbed swiftly down the ladder, and Skip went forward on the upper deck to the wheelhouse. The Magic pulled out of the locks with its bright green seaweed covered walls towering above us, along the shear walls, under the railroad bridge, and out to the channel marked with buoys to keep boats off of the sand spit on our port side.

At the Shilshole entrance buoy, the mate loosened the brake on the tow winch, and the barge began to recede behind us. Skip came back to the aft controls to watch, and when the barge looked like it was the size of a match box, he told the mate to set the brake, and he again went forward to the wheelhouse and increased the Magic's speed. Skip's routine was to then turn the wheel over to the mate while he went to the engine room to make sure that everything was as it should be.

During the trip, Skip explained that the tools of a tugboat are its lines. They are not called ropes (as any boat person knows), because once a length of rope is cut from a coil for use aboard a boat, it becomes a line. The rope used to make tugboat lines is stout stuff. It is heavy to move around, and it is always stowed on deck in coils, ready for use. When the tug is underway, these coils of line must be tied down to a fitting on deck so that they won't wash away.

The success or failure of a landing, especially in difficult weather, can rest on the mate or deckhand's skill at throwing a line; to get that all important first line from the barge made fast to the dock. Then the tug can be freed from the barge, to nudge it the rest of the way to the dock. Skip does it by taking the tug bow-in to the barge, at which time a deckhand puts a line over to the barge and makes it fast to the bow of the tug. Skip then works against that short line, pushing and pulling the barge into place.

Skip talked fondly of the Magic. She was very maneuverable and responsive, excellent characteristics when shifting barges in tight places (what is known in the tugboat industry as juggling). The shape of the Magic's hull gives her an easy motion through the water. Skip has sat comfortably on the aft deck, enjoying a sunny day on the Strait of Georgia, with the wind kicking up a good chop, and watched tugs around him making heavy weather out of the same conditions, spray flying over their decks.

When we returned from Jervis, I told Skip I had felt totally useless, but he was encouraging and said he'd be happy to have me make more trips with him. He told me how to get seaman's papers, so I decided to give it a try.

He put me on the twelve to six watch with the mate; six hours on and six hours off, unless you're the cook. It became my responsibility to make the hourly engine room checks. Skip handed me a pair of ear protectors which I clamped over my ears, and we climbed down the vertical ladder into suffocating heat and the stench of hot lube oil and diesel, and a roar that was merely subdued by the ear muffs. The engine filled the center of the space, rising above our heads, pounding and throwing off tremendous heat. Skip calmly walked around the engine pointing to the gauges and other things that I needed to monitor as I made my rounds. Conversation was out of the question. At the back end of the Fairbanks-Morse engine was a huge, spinning flywheel with guards around it, and aft of that was the shaft alley, with pipe fittings stowed in bins, and tanks suspended along either side. Overhead on the port side was a catwalk decked with expanded steel, and on each side of the engine room sat an auxiliary engine in the widest part of the hull. Along the starboard side was a work bench with tools on pegs within easy reach, and behind that, an air compressor. In every available space were lockers, along the hull and on the forward bulkhead, full of spare parts. Skip's demeanor was one of competence, familiarity, and alertness. When we climbed up the ladder from the engine room, I was never so glad to get out of a place in my life.

The trouble with mates is that they're always hankering for a skipper's job. So it wasn't long before Skip had to find a replacement for Brian. The new mate came aboard and hadn't even stowed his gear when I heard him ask Skip if there was an espresso machine on board. From the look on Skip's face I gathered that it wasn't something he'd ever considered before.

One of the interesting aspects of being on a tugboat with Skip is that he often takes the boat in close to the beach. When we would make a trip north, we would clear the locks, let the tow wire out and after informing Seattle Traffic of Skip's intentions, cross the Vessel Traffic System, or VTS, lanes for the western shore of Puget Sound. Skip would work the Magic along the shoreline so that by the time we were at Point No Point, we could almost shake hands with the fishermen in their waders on the beach by the lighthouse.

While most other commercial vessels stay in the traffic lanes out in the middle of the sound where the tide runs strongest, Skip uses the currents and eddies in close to shore. We never had company in there hugging the beach, unless it was the occasional pleasure boat. Time and again, the Magic would walk away from more powerful tugs out in the middle that were bucking the tide, until they looked like specks in the distance. In the meantime we had a great view of all of the waterfront properties, on what I called Skip's real estate tours. If Skip had any deep sea sailors in the crew, this proximity to land was very unsettling to them. Seattle Traffic griped at him about being out of the VTS traffic lanes, because they wanted everyone who was transiting the sound to do it the same way. Skip put up with the whining and did it his way because it worked, saving him time and fuel.

We had one job in November that seemed like it would be fairly straightforward. We left Seattle around 2:00 P.M. and ran light to Edmonds where we waited for half an hour then took a loaded barge in tow. We were underway by 4:45 P.M. headed north and then east around the south end of Whidbey Island, and north again in Saratoga Passage. By this time it was dark and the Magic was sliding through calm water at an easy seven and a half knots, with the barge out on a short wire.

In Saratoga Passage, Skip saw lots of blips on the radar screen. As we moved closer he switched on the searchlight and we saw many fishboats with a maze of nets stretched out across the channel. Some of the nets did not have lights on them, even though they're supposed to, so we had to look for the floats on the nets, which weren't all that easy to see. Skip had to figure out which net went to what boat, and how to find a way through without damaging any fishnets or colliding with a boat. The fishermen were supposed to shine a light on their nets, but many of the boats appeared dark, as though the entire crew had gone to bed without leaving anyone to stand watch. Skip was focused and unruffled as he delicately picked his way, with a 92' boat and a barge trailing along, through tight twists and turns, somehow threading harmlessly past every obstacle.

With relief we continued on north in clear waters, to the end of the Swinomish Slough where we met the tug Joshua T, the ex-Ruby VIII, which had sunk off of Port Townsend in 1946, towing an empty barge.

After a few exchanged pleasantries with Howard Sullivan, Joshua's skipper, we each let go of our respective barges and traded places. The Joshua T, grabbed hold of the loaded barge and headed into the slough, and we took hold of the empty and started back the way we had come. At the south end of Saratoga Passage Skip, once again, had to thread us through the fishboat maze, and we then proceeded to Edmonds, where we dropped off the barge and headed back to Seattle.

For all of Skip's fondness for the Magic, there were some aspects of her layout that could be challenging to the people on board in rough weather. From the crew's sleeping quarters in the forepeak, and the galley, the head was three doors down on the starboard side deck. When waves would smash over her bow, water would fly the length of the deck, and timing became crucial in order to avoid a cold sea water shower. There was no head on the upper deck, making it very tough on the helmsman in heavy seas, because access to the main deck was by way of the forward ladder, two side ladders, or a climb over the railing and down onto the tow winch.

On December 7, 1992, we had an opportunity to experience how trying this situation could be. We were coming back from Jervis Inlet with a loaded gravel barge. Shortly after coming out of Agamemnon Channel, we encountered ESE winds of thirty knots at Merry Island. Skip decided on a course down the mainland shore, rather than the usual more westerly run down along Vancouver Island, where we would really get clobbered by seas driven by an easterly wind. At Sand Heads, the wind was still blowing easterly. At Point Roberts half an hour before midnight, it was blowing SE at thirty knots, and as we traveled south we began to experience viciously sharp wave action as the wind swept over open water and collided with the ebbing tide. It took us four and a half hours to get abeam of Patos Island, a distance of eleven miles, as the wind cranked up to forty-five and fifty knots SE.

In the Magic it felt like we were in the agitation cycle of a washing machine. The ladder to the crew quarters in the forepeak came loose and rattled around. The coffee pot, held in place by brackets on the stove, jumped free and dumped its contents on the galley deck. Much of what was stowed in the main cabin was thrown into the air and landed on the deck. It was impossible to get down the straight-up-and-down ladder to the engine room, and opening an outside door and going out on deck was not an option.

By the dim light of morning, under heavy, dark clouds, we made our way through the San Juans, getting some relief from the big swell that had built up overnight. The forecast indicated more of the same strong winds, so Skip turned the Magic into Guemes Channel at Anacortes, and headed for the entrance to the Swinomish Slough. We had to take in tow wire before we entered the slough because there is not enough width in the channel for the barge to wander. The barge we had in tow was 180' x 45', and seemed to fill the waterway. Skip was cool and self-assured, making casual comments about some of the boats we passed, accepting a fresh cup of coffee; unfazed by the possibility of calamity from one wrong move.

Skip's dog, Dusty, had become quite a character. Her main area of interest and expertise was the galley; she was what dog trainers would call "food motivated." When she had first come aboard the boats, she had found a cube of butter on the galley table and had helped herself to the whole thing. Since that time, she had acquired boat manners, and understood what she could and could not do. She developed her own routines on the boat and ordered her day around activity in the galley.

She was a delicate little girl with slim legs and long feathers on her front legs and tail, but she would get out on deck where she liked to take naps on dry days, and would start rearranging the big coils of line into a bed. She would paw at those heavy lines and nudge them until she had formed a nest which she would then climb into and go to sleep. Those hard, lumpy lines could not have been very comfortable, but she would snooze curled up in them for hours.

When Dusty would see our preparations for getting the barge through the locks, she would get excited, and once we were underway into the channel, she would take up her position at the top of the forward ladder

DUSTY ASLEEP IN A COIL OF LINE ON THE AFT DECK.

DUSTY WAITING FOR THE ACTION TO BEGIN.

COMING INTO THE LOCKS WITH THE GRAVEL BARGE ALONGSIDE. DUSTY SUPERVISING FROM HER USUAL SPOT AT THE BOW OF THE MAGIC.

DUSTY DISAPPOINTED TO SEE AN EMPTY GALLEY.

SKIP CHECKING THE ENGINE'S COOLING WATER OUTFLOW.

ahead of the wheelhouse where she could see what was happening. As we would enter the lock chamber, Dusty would go down to the foredeck and put her front feet up on the bulwarks, as though she was keeping an eye on Skip's barge handling techniques. One of the lock attendants that Skip called the "mayor of Steilacoom," always had dog biscuits and a friendly word ready when we reached the fresh water level.

Over the years, Dusty gained an appreciation for good food that would sometimes cause Skip to put her on a diet. During one such period, he had put down a bowl of dry kibble in front of her, and he had gone into the living room where he sat in his favorite chair, looking out at the water. Not one to hide her disgust, Dusty walked out of the kitchen and came over to him with her mouth full of dog food, and spit it out at his feet, then turned around and walked away.

Skip would set our departure times for the trips to Jervis based on the tides. He always tried to get us to the pit well before daylight, so that we would be first to load, because whoever was first to arrive would be able to tie to the dock and be loaded without delay in the morning.

One night we were coming out of Agamemnon Channel at about three A.M., just a few miles from the pit. There was a Canadian tug behind us, and as we left the narrow channel that led into the more open waters of Jervis Inlet, it became apparent that the other tug was trying to overtake us in order to get to the dock ahead of us. Skip told me to start the winch engine and let it warm up, without being obvious about it. With the autopilot steering, we went back to the tow winch and began taking in wire on the fly. Usually we would slow down to a sedate pace when we brought in the tow wire, but this time we were racing.

Skip stood at the winch in his usual nonchalant stance, but his eyes were burning. The tow wire spooled onto the winch drum without a hitch, and the barge barreled along right behind us. Skip slowed the Magic down gradually, and was happy to see the Canadian tug back down and take in their tow wire in a more orthodox manner. We had the barge positioned under the loading shute when they finally showed up. There is no waiting pier at the pit, so the Canadians had to do donuts out in the bay until we left six hours later.

Skip is so quick and sure-footed that, when he senses hesitation in one of the crew, he is down the ladder from the wheelhouse, taking the line, up on the barge to the bitt, back on the boat and making the line fast, and back up to the wheelhouse in the blink of an eye.

His way of doing things, making up to a barge, for example, has evolved as he has discovered what works for him. In his wheelhouse briefing of the crew before docking or taking a barge alongside, he will tell them what he intends to do and what he needs from them. Time after time, experienced tugboat men, new to Skip's crew, will invariably respond that they've never done it that way, that you can't do that.

He is always in tune with the pulse of the boat, as well as the forces of wind, water, and momentum which he uses to his advantage whenever possible, rather than just muscling through with sheer horsepower. He has the confidence born of trust in his instincts and experience, to go into any situation and feel that he can handle whatever develops. It is this unwavering confidence in his abilities, and his talent for attunement with the tug, even boats deemed hard to handle, that is evident in his boat handling. His total awareness of his surroundings, and his visualization of cause and effect, eight moves ahead of the one he's engaged in, keep surprises to a minimum. Most crew members do not possess this ability, and must be open to his direction and focused on his next signal, or shout, as the case may be. Skip's crew would do well to leave their egos at home in their sock drawers before making a trip with him.

Something that becomes evident to anyone on Skip's tugboats for any length of time is his familiarity with every aspect of the boat. If it's not working right, he can tweak it; if it's broken, he can fix it.

I began to realize this two months after joining the Magic's crew. We had run light to Elliott Bay and up the Duwamish River to pick up our barge for a trip to Jervis. We took the barge in tow and had gotten no farther than West Point, five miles north of Elliott Bay, when the Fairbanks engine began having problems. We left the barge on the south buoy in Shilshole Bay, and Skip limped the Magic back to her moorings.

He rescheduled the trip, and the mate and seaman went home.

While waiting for the engine to cool down, Skip determined what the trouble was. Since the other crew members had not offered assistance, I told Skip I'd give him a hand, not that I'd be much help. When I showed up at the boat later, Skip had the covers off of the top of the engine, and they were set out of the way on the catwalk. He said that he needed to replace a liner. This entailed lifting the upper crankshaft, to which he had already attached chain hoists. We winched the long, cumbersome part out of the way by standing on the top of the open engine, and cranking the three chain hoists. Skip walked easily around the narrow edges of the open engine from one hoist to the next. When the crankshaft was secured out of the way, the upper and lower piston and rod assemblies had to be removed. The lower assembly was 33" long and too heavy for most people to lift, but Skip wrestled the ungainly thing out. After disconnecting some fittings, Skip threaded in two eyebolts at the top of the liner. He attached chain hoists to the eyes, and we began to take up slack, but the liner was stuck in the hole. Skip worked his way through his lexicon of salty words, including "Balderdash and the queen of the May," whatever that meant.

Skip's determination and perseverance won out over the recalcitrance of the liner, and we hoisted the big, heavy milk can looking thing over to the catwalk along the port side of the engine. The new liner, just as cranky about going in as the old one was about coming out, finally succumbed to all of Skip's tricks, and everything was reinserted and assembled. Over his twelve year relationship with this engine, Skip had become, by necessity, quite expert at keeping it running.

The Fairbanks-Morse Opposed Piston engine requires that a slight vacuum be maintained in the crankcase, when the engine is running, for it to operate properly. There is a vacuum gauge mounted in plain sight on the aft end of the engine to monitor this. Certain factors can generate pressure in the engine, one symptom of which is that the engine begins to drool oil. A much more dramatic indication of pressure occurs when the engine has a base explosion. One of the twenty doors through which pistons are replaced blows off with a loud Boosh, at such velocity that it is dented by the impact. All hell breaks loose, as fire and hot oil belch out of the engine. Skip has had to run down, on more than one occasion, into this inferno and shut down the engine, replace the door, and restart the engine. After a base explosion, when I had to make the hourly engine room checks, the hair on the back of my neck would stand up as I thought about the effects of one of those flying steel doors being propelled at high speed into the soft flesh of a human body.

Whenever we would bring a load of gravel from Jervis Inlet, we would always take on our usual passengers. Seagulls never failed to hitch a ride on the piles of gravel. We probably transported many illegal seagull aliens across the U.S. border in this manner. They would all have flown away by the time we neared our destination. They always left us many presents, though. As we climbed over the barge and across the piles of gravel, getting lines set up for our landing, we would get covered in white seagull droppings.

At Golden Gardens beach to the north of Shilshole Marina, we would shorten up the tow wire. We would then throw off the towing bridles, and Skip would whip the tug around to the side of the barge, and we would make up to it for the trip through the locks. It's necessary to have fairly calm water for this maneuver, so Skip would keep an eye out for large ships barreling down the sound at twenty knots, throwing huge wakes. We still caught a couple of them when there was a lot of traffic, which would lift the barge and tug and bang them loudly together, with the crew right in the middle of it; the barge rolling and its decks awash.

One morning we came in with a loaded barge and ran into a thick pocket of fog over Shilshole Bay. We were getting ready to make up to the barge when we saw a shape ghost out of the swirling mist. It was a sailboat, and then there was another one, barely discernable. We were in the midst of sailboats jockeying for position at the start of a race. We messed up some race tactics that morning.

Another time, we were making up to the barge in the same spot, with the mate on the barge to secure lines from the tug. A Kvichak fishing boat came tearing out from the direction of the locks, with lots of people on board. It was obviously new, and it looked like they were out for sea trials. For some reason they tore past us just feet away. Then they ran in circles around us, kicking up a wake that smashed the tug and barge together. We yelled at them that they were putting us in danger, but they just ignored us. All we could do was back away and wait for them to leave, and let the water calm down.

The beach off of Golden Gardens Park next to Shilshole Marina stretches north for miles in a gentle sandy arc. Just inland of the beach, trains run on an elevated track, separating the long expanse of sand from houses and parks on the other side. On a dark night, Skip and his crew were in close to the shore. The deckhand saw the headlight of a locomotive coming in their direction down the tracks. He shouted in terror that the train was going to run them down.

The entrance to the locks has an adjoining fish ladder for returning salmon and becomes a focal point for fishermen, commercial and recreational, as well as sea lions, during salmon runs. A long spit juts out from Magnolia Bluff, requiring precise navigation of the buoys, providing minimal maneuvering room should something occur, such as a yacht owner stopping dead in front of us in the middle of the restricted channel to go aft and adjust the length of his dinghy painter.

Skip has had to blast the danger signal repeatedly, when knots of sportsfishermen in small boats were congregated near the Shilshole Bay entrance buoy, blocking the channel; moving ever so grudgingly at the last possible moment as we bore down on them at dead slow with the barge lumbering behind us.

One sparkling April day, we made up to our barge on the ship canal, and headed out through the locks. When we rounded the spit on the north end of Magnolia, we took our first look at Shilshole Bay. White sails flashed in the sunlight all across the bay before us, in what was obviously a big sailboat race. The wind was fresh, blowing about twenty knots out of the west/southwest, the light chop dazzling with refracted light - a sea of diamonds.

In order to get clear of the sailboats massed outside of the marina breakwater, Skip set a course due west into the only part of the bay not cluttered with boats, once we passed the entrance buoy. This put us parallel to the nearest racers who were beating to windward on our starboard side. We let out some tow wire and watched as the barge eased away behind us a short distance. At this point, the bluffs of Discovery Park rose abeam of us, and West Point was ahead and to port. At our speed of eight knots, we would get free of the pack, then turn north toward the VTS buoy, Sierra Foxtrot.

There were four boats sailing close-hauled, just forward of our starboard bow. We were stunned when the nearest boat headed up, with no warning, as the wind veered southerly, and sheeted in on a course directly across our bow. Four crew members stared at us from their perch on the windward side rail of the boat, with their legs dangling against the hull as they slid past our bow fender with only feet to spare.

Skip wrenched the throttle back just in time to avoid a collision. The tug slowed, but the empty barge surged ahead. We watched in utter disbelief as three more boats replicated this maneuver in front of us. There was no stopping the onslaught of the barge, churning along on our port side. The crew members on these boats just sat on the rail, legs hanging down, watching the barge charging at them. If the wind had faltered by so much as a knot, these sailors would have gone to the great sailboat race in the sky; their bodies washing up on shore along with chunks of tattered fiberglass, in front of the West Point sewage treatment plant.

The Lakeside Industries towing contract put Skip smack in the middle of Seattle's busy boating scene. Where the Duwamish was used mostly by commercial traffic, the ship canal – from the locks to Lake Washington – was the playground of Seattle's numerous pleasure boats. Some of these boaters lose sight of the fact that the canal is also a commercial waterway. Add to that the fact that some people buy a boat and operate it without knowing the Coast Guard's Rules of Navigation relating to a restricted channel. These rules apply to all vessels: powerboats, sailboats, rowboats, fishing boats.

Stay as close as possible to the edge of the channel on your starboard side.

Do not impede the progress of vessels navigating in the channel.

Power and sailboats must stay out of the way of vessels restricted in maneuverability.

Vessels required to stay out of the way must take early and substantial action to keep well clear. The other vessel will maintain her course and speed.

Do not impede traffic while fishing in the channel.

Ignorance of these rules can initiate some harrowing experiences for these boaters when they encounter a large vessel in a narrow channel. The results are about what you would get if you bought a car and began driving it without at least reading a driver's manual.

This was demonstrated over and over when we would come in with a loaded barge for Lakeside. The plant's location made it necessary for us to cross the canal and make a landing with the barge on our port side. If there was opposing traffic, which there usually was in good weather, Skip would blow a passing signal indicating his intention to pass starboard to starboard. Boaters have only four whistle signals that they need to know:

- 1 short blast – altering course to starboard
- 2 short blasts – altering course to port
- 3 short blasts – backing astern
- 5 (or more) short blasts – warning of potential danger. In doubt as to intentions of opposing traffic.

Skip would begin working the barge to the other shore of the canal. As the gap would begin to close, boaters would speed up to try to make it through the diminishing slot. If they had understood his signal, they would have comprehended his intentions and acknowledged by repeating the signal and going to port, avoiding a big drama. As it was, Skip would have to blow the danger signal, which they would not understand, but they would begin to sense the urgency of the signal and realize that they were rapidly running out of room, and could possibly be squashed like a bug, so they would veer off at the last moment looking pale and nervous. The crew would stand on the bow of the tug and the barge, and yell and signal with their arms, but those boaters kept on coming like sheep to the slaughter.

Our landing was complicated one morning by the presence of a novice rowing team in one of Seattle Pacific University's rowing shells. The college is across the canal from the Lakeside plant, and they liked to use that stretch of water for rowing practice. On this gray March morning, they were paying no heed to our approach as they straddled the middle of the canal, like one of those water strider bugs that skate on ponds. The instructor was accompanying his students in a Boston Whaler. Skip blew the danger signal, and those five loud blasts of the Magic's whistle resounded in the still morning air.

As I raised my binoculars to get a better look, there was a disjointed stutter of oars as the scull slued sharply. The boat rolled and in seconds was floating upside down. The oars drifted lazily in every direction, as heads began to pop up around the overturned hull. The timbre of the engine changed as Skip throttled back to slow us down. The decrease in speed was negligible as the momentum of the barge pulled us forward.

The attending Boston Whaler squirreled around ineffectually as we bore down on them. Again, the danger signal blasted across the water. The nine unwitting swimmers splashed frantically, while the two people in the Whaler skidded about, busily trying to capture the wayward oars. They were not recognizing the peril they were in.

By this time, we were close enough to these people to communicate vocally, shouting at them to forget the damned oars and concentrate on clearing everybody out of our way. As we loomed larger on their diminished horizon, they began to get the picture. The swimmers, who must have been numb with cold, were rounded up and herded, finally, to the south bank of the canal. We overtook them as we maintained our course along the north shore, gliding by without further incident; a bunch of soggy college kids bobbing gently in our wake.

Inlet Marine was hired for a dredge tending job in the summer of

1993 for A.H. Powers Company. The contractor would be removing sediment from the Cedar River, where it flowed into Lake Washington by the Boeing Renton plant. The dredging had to be accomplished without disrupting salmon runs, so they started work in early July when they wouldn't bother the fish.

Our involvement began when we went to the A.H. Powers yard on the Blair Waterway in Tacoma, to pick up some of the equipment that would be used at the job site. Skip directed us to lash the barges together, and we took them to Seattle. At 10:20 that night we hung the dump scow on the south buoy in Shilshole Bay, outside the locks, and towed a crane barge through the locks and into the canal.

The barge's crane boom and spuds (the things that are lowered into the mud to anchor it) stuck up so high that we had to have all of the drawbridges opened for us. Since it was after 11:00 P.M., Skip called the one bridge attendant on duty to let him know we were leaving the locks, so that he could come and open the Ballard Bridge for us. We had to wait for him to drive to the bridge and then open it. After we were through, he closed it and drove to the Fremont Bridge, opened and closed it, and raced to the University Bridge. Skip had the Magic slowed way down, but we had to wait at each bridge. Then the bridge attendant jumped in his car and roared off to open the Montlake Bridge for us. Once clear of the drawbridges, we proceeded on to Lake Washington. Because of the height of the barge, we had to have the Evergreen Point Floating Bridge open for us, as well. We waited for an hour and forty minutes as they tried to open the span, had a malfunction had to close it, and try it again. It was 02:45 A.M. when we finally made it through the opening. We handed off the barge to A.H. Powers' tug, Double Eagle, and went back to pick up the dump scow tethered outside the locks. It wasn't until 08:30 A.M. that we had the barge made fast in Renton.

Once the Powers crew began digging, we towed the dump scow loaded with dredge spoils to the designated dump site, which was in Elliott Bay. It was a four hour trip from the south end of Lake Washington to the locks. Once we were through the locks, it took another two and a half hours to reach the dump site at the south end of Elliott Bay, off of

Todd Shipyards. The mate, Dave Gudgell, would get the engine on the barge warmed up in preparation for the dump.

The dump site was closely monitored by the Coast Guard. We had to use a Global Positioning System to locate the exact spot, and be in contact with the Coast Guard who would authorize us to begin, when they agreed that we were indeed on the target. There was a nasty hot spot of chemical pollution from years of industrial runoff at the bottom of the bay and the idea was to cover it with clean dredge material.

The mate would open the dogs on the barge at Skip's signal, and the material would begin to fall through the opened hoppers. You would think that the rocks and gravel would just fall out, but Skip would have to take the barge in tight circles to get the materials to release, while staying over the designated spot. I monitored the GPS to make sure we stayed within the required coordinates. The barge, when loaded, was about the height of the Magic's aft deck. As it began to free itself of its load, it would jump up, and by the time it was empty, Dave had a pretty good climb down the ladder that I would set in place to get him back aboard the tug.

An interesting aspect of this dump site was that it was right next to, if not actually in, the ferry lanes. As the ferry would come in, it would swerve out of its course to stay clear of us. The wakes were useful, though, to knock the clinging mud out of the barge.

Once we had emptied and closed up the barge, we headed back to Renton so that the dredging crew could fill it again. We would then tie up the Magic nearby and get some sleep.

The dump scow loaded with dredge spoils draws about 14' and has a beam of 55'. The Montlake cut was usually the most troublesome part of the trip because it is very narrow with sloping concrete sides and when there is any traffic through there at all, there are some pretty sporty sea conditions. I've been on white water rafting trips that were calmer.

On one trip in from the lake with the loaded dump scow, we had committed ourselves to the cut when one of these pumpkin seed twenty-footers with its bow way up in the air so that we can't see the driver, which probably means he can't see us, even if we are 30' tall and 55' wide, came into the other end of the cut. The water was just a-boiling and this little boat was rocking and rolling all over the place. Skip gave him a blast of the danger signal, which is pretty impressive echoing off all that cement. As we drew closer together, we saw that he had a bunch of little kids with him. We sounded the danger signal again in the hope that he would turn around, but we continued to converge. He aimed that little eggshell of a boat between the steel tug and barge and the concrete wall, into the turmoil of narrow water. The kids were clinging, wide-eyed, to seats and railings, while mom braced herself, stiff and pale, clutching a toddler in her lap. The guy gave us a big smile and a wave as we passed. I guess he thought we were just being friendly with all that whistle tooting.

One night we were making a run from the lake to Puget Sound with the loaded dump barge. As we rounded Webster Point, there were no boat running lights ahead of us as we lined up on the buoys, so it appeared that we had a clear shot through the cut. The Montlake cut, at night, is a featureless black hole backlit by lights on the other end. As we came closer to the bridge, there seemed to be an even blacker hole in the surrounding darkness. Skip flashed the beam of the searchlight into the cut. There, waiting for the bridge to open, was a sailboat with no lights showing. After five blasts of the tug's whistle, a head snapped up through the companionway hatch. Skip had to make a slight course change to get around him. Skip asked him, while thundering past what in the world he had been thinking of, sitting there with no lights on. He shouted back that he was conserving his batteries. That would have been interesting engraved on his tombstone.

One black August night we were on our way into Lake Washington with the empty dump scow in tow. At the approach to the cut, we scanned the water with binoculars and searchlight. We picked out three small dots on the water under the bridge that could have been ducks, but we'd seen this movie before, so we watched carefully. In the beam of light we discerned a human face. Two of the floating heads moved to the side of the canal. The third guy, splayed out on his back in mid channel, was totally oblivious to our approach. A tugboat, which is not exactly a stealth machine with its throbbing engines and huge thrashing propellor rarely succeeds in sneaking up on anyone. The floater failed

> THE QUARRY AT LUMMI ISLAND, BELLINGHAM BAY IN THE BACKGROUND. MAGIC IS TIED TO A LOADED BARGE THAT IS OUT OF TRIM, WHICH MEANS IT NEEDS MORE LOAD IN THE BOW TO EVEN IT OUT.

> NOVEMBER IN JERVIS INLET. MAGIC AT THE PIT WHILE THE BARGE IS BEING LOADED.

to move, and it wasn't until Skip had played him a lengthy rendition of get-the-heck-out-of-the-way with the tug's whistle that he flipped over and dog paddled to safety.

We made the run from the Cedar River to Elliott Bay, from July 7th to September 15th, forty-seven times with the dump scow, requiring ninety-four lock passages and trips through the ship canal. Skip, Dave, and I had our nervous systems on full alert the whole time. We kept an eye on the pleasure boats, which Skip called "toy boats," that were all around us as we made our way up and down the canal. Skip's alert attention to the circus of activity in the crowded waterways kept the thoughtless, the clueless, and the beer addled boaters out of harm's way. As we would approach the locks with the loaded dump scow, small boats would dart ahead of us and tie up to the shear wall at the lock entrance. The lock master would have to get on the P.A. system and tell them to move for their own safety. Occasionally someone in a big, expensive yacht would take exception to the fact that commercial traffic has priority in the locks (even on nice sunny days) and the lock master would have to tell them loudly to get out of our way and wait their turn.

Going through the locks during summer tourist season felt a lot like being part of a zoo exhibit. People would hang on the railing, watching our every move.

Skip was unflappable, bringing the barge in smoothly, joking with some of the lock attendants, and answering questions put to him by curious onlookers. We became a standard feature at the locks twice a day, five days a week, for ten weeks that summer.

Because we were busy with the dump scow run during the week, we would have to fit trips to Jervis and Steilacoom in on weekends to keep Lakeside supplied with gravel and sand.

As if that wasn't enough pressure, the engine was giving us fits. Several times we had to tie up at Lakeside and bring pistons on board, which we installed when we were at Renton waiting for the barge to be loaded.

Skip has a recurring dream that he's in the Magic and he has a barge on a long tow wire. He is towing the barge on the freeway, and his exit is coming up and he's trying to figure out how to make it down the off ramp without taking out a bunch of cars with the barge. It's easy to see where that dream might have come from.

At 06:00 A.M. on October 24, 1993, Skip and his crew assembled aboard the Magic. We had a new mate with us, an Oregon fisherman with a little tugboat experience. The barge we needed for the job was in Tacoma, so we ran south to pick it up. At the Blair Waterway we had to wait for the low car bridge to open, in order to get to the A.H. Powers yard where the barge was tied up. The barge looked like it was down by the bow, so Skip and the mate opened hatches to find out where the water was. They hoisted the gas powered scow pump up onto the barge and lowered a hose into the pocket of water, and began pumping it out over the side.

If a person doesn't know what they're doing, this procedure can kill them. A barge must be opened up and air allowed to circulate through the hull before it is safe to enter the hull. To just open a hatch and climb down into a barge is certain death. There have been cases where a man went into a barge, and after a while someone would wonder where he went, and go looking for him. They would eventually look into the open hatch on the barge and see the crumpled form of the man. Not knowing the danger from the lack of oxygen they would climb hastily down the ladder to their own death.

There was quite a lot of water in the barge, and after an hour of pumping, there was still water in it. So we made up to the barge and headed out with the scow pump still spewing a hefty stream at 11:00 A.M. When the pump ran dry, Skip and the mate pulled up the hose, dogged the hatch covers, and stowed the scow pump, and we continued north, letting out tow wire for a run to Jervis Inlet.

The barge we were towing was identified as the 203, but we called it the barge from hell. It was just a big steel box with a flat bottom. The builder had not put skegs on it, which would have provided directional stability, so it towed erratically.

The weather was calm and the tides were not extreme. Even at Point Partridge there was no westerly swell, so the trip was easy and pleasant. I stayed in the wheelhouse with the new mate on the midnight to six watch, to familiarize him with the route as we wound through the San Juan Islands.

Soft fall sunlight suffused the morning as we made good time over the smooth gray blue waters of the Strait of Georgia. Skip and I were in the wheelhouse enjoying the tranquility of a post-breakfast cup of coffee around 08:45 when we were startled by a tremendous PA-WUMPH from below. The doors to the engine room were open to let in cool morning air and smoke billowed out of every door. Skip bounded down the ladder to the main deck. The smoke was too dense to see anything, but down the ladder he went into the engine room, to shut down the engine and make sure there was no fire.

It took a while for the smoke to clear because there was not a breath of wind. When Skip was able to see, he found that the Fairbanks had had one heck of a base explosion. Oil was sprayed on every surface in the engine room. As Skip investigated and probed into the engine with his light, he discovered that the lower crankshaft was broken. He came topside and said "We're done."

We set about winching ourselves back to the barge with the towline and made the Magic fast to the barge (an ironic term, under the circumstances).

Skip called Mariner Towing, a Canadian outfit, to see if they had a tug available to tow us home. They said they would send a boat, but it would take a while. Since we were about eleven miles from Merry Island and only forty miles from the pit at Jervis, Skip decided to have the tug take us up to load the barge so that he would at least have income from the trip. When the tug, Sealane, arrived, Skip told them what he wanted them to do, and they put their towline on the barge, and they towed us, with the Magic tied alongside the barge, to the gravel pit. The Sealane was small, about 70' with cramped quarters for the four man crew, but she had the horsepower to pull the loaded barge away from the dock. With the Magic being on the end of the towline next to the barge, it was quiet. We had a generator running, but compared to the roar of a Fairbanks, it was hardly noticeable, mingled with the shoosh of water flowing past the two hulls.

We went through Agamemnon Channel on a short tow line and it was a weird ride because this was the barge from hell. It would sheer off to one side of the narrow channel, spin and head for the other side, back and forth with the Magic tied to the starboard side aft. About the time we thought we were going to smack into the rocky bank, it would turn and charge off in the other direction. The Canadian skipper had a few comments to Skip over the VHS radio about the barge's towing characteristics. Once we threaded our way between the narrow confines of Pearson Island on the port side and an outcropping of rocks to starboard, the crew of the Sealane let out tow wire, and before long they looked to us like a small bathtub toy.

It could have been quite relaxing to let someone else do the work. Dusty thought it was great. The barge, when loaded, was level with the Magic's deck, and I would pick her up and set her over on the gravel. She would tear up one pile, over the top and down to the valley between the mounds, joyful to be on something that smelled like the earth. It would have been a laid back cruise, free of hourly engine room checks. But there was Skip. He was beside himself. The Magic had done herself in.

He called his insurance company with the news of the broken crankshaft. The conversation was disheartening; they didn't think the crankshaft loss would be covered. Everything hinged, or unhinged, on the decision of the insurance company. And there he was, going about five knots down the Strait of Georgia, tied to the barge from hell.

We had hardly gotten into open water when a thick, wooly blanket of fog descended over us. It was so dense that we could no longer see the tug in front of us. We went the entire trip without ever seeing the tug, or anything else for that matter, watching the Magic's radar to see where we were, and if the Canadians were keeping us off the beach. We talked about the engine's increasingly troublesome behavior. Maybe the crankshaft had been cracked for some time. We had changed at least ten pistons in the fifteen months I had worked on the Magic. We had become so practiced at it that Skip and I would take our cups of coffee down to the engine room with us, set up the special Fairbanks winches on each side of the piston hole, and remove the damaged piston. We would pour ourselves another cup of coffee and set up for the installation of the new piston. Skip would get the unwieldy piston with the rod flopping around into the hole. The assembly was very heavy and he had to do this at arm's length. I would be on the other side of the engine with a bolt ready to insert into the upper piece of the piston rod and through the rod, which held the bearings in place around the crankshaft. Understandably, Skip would be anxious to let go of all of that weight as quickly as possible, so it was a little intense. I would thread a nut onto the bolt to hold everything in place. We would get the other bolt into place with its nuts, and insert cotter pins, all of this taking place on our knees looking into a smallish hole and doing some of it by feel. We would have it done in an hour and a half.

When we reached Seattle, Skip hit the ground running. The insurance company had to be dealt with, estimates had to be made, and replacement boats had to be looked at, just in case. The gang at Hatch & Kirk, the Fairbanks-Morse dealer, murmured sympathetically as they put together a repair cost estimate for their long-time customer. The news was devastating; the crankshaft alone, excluding any labor, would cost $88,666.02. I asked Skip if he thought they'd consider knocking off the two cents since he was such a good customer. To even get to the lower crankshaft, the entire engine would have to be dismantled.

We walked docks in a dispirited mood looking at tugs that had languished at their moorings for far too long. It was a bleak exercise.

The insurance company harumphed and sputtered for a week, as insurance companies are wont to do. The bill came in from the Canadians for the towing, which ate up the proceeds from the trip. And everyone that knew anything about Fairbanks-Morse Opposed Piston engines scratched their heads and said the same thing; the lower crankshaft never breaks; it's totally unheard of.

The decision of the insurance company was that an engine replacement would far exceed the value of the boat, so the Magic was declared a total loss.

They grudgingly sent Skip a check. With the check in the mail,

Skip began to look in earnest for another boat. Amazingly, there was an ex-Navy tug lying just across the canal from the Magic's moorings. Skip decided to check it out. There was no electricity to the tug, so we looked around in the darkness of the cavernous engine room, aided by the weak beams of our flashlights. Dave Updike, the owner, had died several months before and his wife was anxious to divest herself of all of his marine holdings. After looking the tug over, we realized that she was in fabulous shape, she just looked terrible. Someone had painted her with incompatible paints and she was peeling like a bad sunburn. The wife was so eager to sell, that Skip didn't have a chance to make an offer before her agent called and quoted him a very reasonable price. Skip, who had been prepared to offer her more, agreed to buy the tug.

JERVIS INLET WINDS THROUGH THIS MOUNTAINOUS TERRAIN. THE BARGE IS NEAR THE ENTRANCE TO AGA-

MEMNON CHANNEL. THE TOW WIRE WAS LET OUT FOR THE TRIP BACK TO SEATTLE.

CHAPTER SEVENTEEN

By early November, Skip had taken possession of the 102' ex-Navy tug. She had been built in 1945 at Terminal Island, California, by the Bethlehem Steel Company, as YTB-702, and named the USS Arawak. She had a beam of 25' 9 ½" and a draft of 11' 3 ½". By the time she was finished World War II had ended, and she was laid up without ever being commissioned. Her hull below the water line was fendered with wide strips of rubber, called submarine rubber, for tending subs. In 1967 she was put into service for the first time. She was used as a training vessel in San Diego and Long Beach, and had a few dents to prove it. The Navy had sold her to Dave Updike. He, in turn, had sold her and she had gone to Petersburg, Alaska, with the name Confident. That had not gone too well, apparently, because Updike had repossessed the boat and brought her back to Seattle.

Skip chose to name her the Michael, in memory of his son who had died twenty-one years before.

We had no time to lose. We had to transfer tools and equipment from the Magic to the Michael. Skip spent his time figuring out the tug's elaborate systems, and getting the Cleveland diesel engines to rumble to life. They were original equipment, forerunners of the modern EMD engines. The boat had a diesel-electric system, each engine having its own generator and, combined, producing 1300 h.p.

The two of us slaved like dogs, getting the boat ready. This is possibly not an apt phrase because, Dusty, the dog, on the other hand, lounged on her bed and yawned as she watched us work. Everything on a tugboat is heavy; so much so that some of the big chunks had to be winched from boat to boat, from the bowels of one to the bowels of the other, time and time again.

The Michael had no tow winch, and Skip loved the winch on the Magic, so he fabricated a winch base from two H-beams he lowered onto the aft deck and set in place. The weather turned bitterly cold, and we tarped the winch area to allow us to keep working. When the base was welded into place and painted, a crane came and transferred the tow winch to the Michael.

I painted her new name on her bow, and on December 5, she made her first trip for Inlet Marine. The mate came back from Oregon after a month and a half off, and we made a run to Everett to pick up a barge and take it to Steilacoom for a load of sand and back to Lakeside; a nice little shakedown cruise.

The next day, we began her second trip, up to Jervis Inlet for gravel. The boat was unfamiliar, the engine room was huge and complicated, and we brought along an unstable deckhand/cook with us, because Skip was hard-pressed to find another person. The barometer reading at the beginning of the trip was 29.50, dropping steadily through the night. By the time we reached Merry Island, it had dipped to 29.15 and we were rolling in the slop of a twenty-five knot easterly.

We reached the pit and tied to the loading dock at 10:00 P.M. and loaded the next morning. By the time we headed out through Agamemnon Channel, Skip was hearing radio transmissions from boats in the strait that things were going from bad to worse. At noon, still a mile and a half from the channel entrance, we were feeling storm force winds out of the south/southeast. The water in the channel was in an uproar, so Skip elected to tie to some log booms in an indentation in the rocky shoreline euphemistically called Boom Bay. We tied a line from the tug to the logs, and then Skip walked aft on the surging log raft to attach a line to the barge. It was wild and he wouldn't let anyone off of the boat to help him. With everything secured to the logs, we hoped they were well tied to shore. We stood watches, the pilot house windows shaking violently through the night with each hurricane force gust.

The next morning at seven Skip stuck the Michael's bow into Malaspina Strait, and we bucked a heavy swell, but the wind had calmed and

THE MICHAEL COMING INTO THE LOCKS WITH A BARGE.

THE BARGE SNUGGED UP TO THE STERN OF THE TUG. CREW IS HANDLING THE TOWING BRIDLES DURING DESCENT IN THE LOCKS.

GAIL MASSOTH

the barometer was back up to 29.52. The weather and sea conditions continued to moderate as we moved south.

After plowing through typical December slop on a couple of subsequent trips, it was a pleasant change to head out of Seattle, running light for Indian Island across from Port Townsend. We arrived at 10:15 A.M. and Skip received instructions for a submarine tending job. At 11:00 we departed for our assigned position off of Hein Bank, five miles south of San Juan Island. If there had been any weather blowing westerly or southerly, we would have been exposed. But it was a placid January day, with roaming patches of fog, in a weak wash of sunlight.

We sat in the wheelhouse and drank coffee and munched on pastries. Phil Shively, who owned his own tugboat, had been persuaded to make the trip, so he and Skip swapped stories. We saw the submarine surface once, which was entertaining.

After drifting around for four hours, the Navy called on the radio to say that they were done with their tests, and we were free to go. We ate dinner while cruising back to Seattle under clear skies.

Skip was having a difficult time finding a mate, so he prevailed on Phil Shively to make another trip with us in late February, this time to Jervis Inlet. On the trip north, we were able to go west of the San Juan Islands by way of Haro Strait, and through Active Pass, to the Strait of Georgia; a desirable route only in mild weather.

Haro Strait separates the San Juans from the cluster of small Canadian Islands off of Vancouver Island to the west. Above San Juan Island, Stuart Island protrudes into Haro Strait and at its northern end there is a light on Turn Point, which we passed to starboard at about 9:30 P.M. We headed northwest into the lower Canadian Gulf Islands along Swanson Channel for four miles, and then on a more northerly course into a narrower channel. In the dark, it started to feel claustrophobic, with the barge trailing along, as the land began to close in.

The entrance to Active Pass is totally obscured so that it looks like the skipper has taken leave of his senses and is going to crash the tug into a high black land mass. We had shortened the tow wire and slowly moved toward the looming island. Out of the black ahead of us rumbled a huge shape, startling for all of its lights suddenly blazing from windows above us. The B.C. ferry charged on by us, and when it was clear of the barge, Skip took the Michael steadily forward and began a turn to starboard into the pass which then took a sharp bend to starboard.

For a mile the tug bounced around in lively currents which, in the daylight, are fished by eagles. Then the boat made a 90 degree turn to port and squeezed through a slot between the island and shoals for a couple of miles. Suddenly we emerged into open water ahead of us, and we let out tow wire as we turned north to head into the strait.

After loading the barge at the pit, we encountered a moderate to heavy swell with winds southeast at twenty-five knots, when we left the protection of Agamemnon Channel for the return trip. Through the night the wind blew easterly and then switched to westerly and began to pick up in intensity. The weather grew meaner by the hour. The seas were so sharp, and the Michael's action through the waves was so violent, that everything that we had so carefully stowed, broke out of lockers. Heavy steel galley drawers vomited up all of their contents onto the deck, and dishes and glasses broke free and shattered. Everything on the deck slid from side to side with a crash as we were tossed around.

Getting down the stairs to the engine room was accomplished by hanging on for dear life, descending the steep ladder backward, and keeping a low center of gravity. Tools were thrown on the deck from heavy drawers that sat in notches to (supposedly) keep them from opening in heavy weather. While lurching from one hand hold to the next, and trying to keep my footing, I would stagger around the engine room reading gauges and making sure that the cooling water day tank was full. The engine room was still set up in Navy style, which meant each engine had a day tank with a sight gauge on it for fuel. These tanks required filling every couple of hours or the engines would die for lack of fuel. Therefore it was imperative that I made hourly engine room checks, or we would have been in trouble. The boat was set up for a crew of at least eight men, and in these conditions it was a real handful.

We had two dogs on board; Dusty, and a male English Setter named Bandit, who was not accustomed to boats and was used to having the floor remain stationary under his feet. They were doing their best to remain upright, with legs splayed out, wild-eyed and breathing fast. As the boat pitched and rolled, they would slide and hit the bulkhead, and then slide and slam into the opposite bulkhead, along with the rest of the debris on the deck. I captured each dog, stuffing them into Skip's bunk and surrounding them with pillows and blankets, then closed the door to his stateroom. I had vivid flashes of dogs with broken legs and deep bleeding gashes in their paws.

Reaching the upper end of Rosario Strait, we immediately felt some relief in the lee of Orcas Island, but it was still rough. As we proceeded down Rosario, the wind kept building. At Burrows Island we were beginning to feel the force of the storm again, so we took in tow wire and lumbered through the little pass between Fidalgo and Burrows Islands in the dark at 06:10 A.M. We had to mill around in Burrows Bay for two hours, waiting for the tide to slacken so that we could make a run for it through Deception Pass. As we waited, the wind notched up to sixty knots with higher gusts, and the waves that had been battering Whidbey Island marched along the shoreline and into our little bay. We would have to cross three miles of open water to get to the pass.

It was a wild ride those three miles, the barge wallowing in heavy seas. As Skip swung the tug and barge into alignment with the pass, we were suddenly and violently awash in beam seas, which was spectacularly demonstrated by the barge which took big, pendulous rolls from side to side on the short towline just off of our stern. We plunged into the pass, lifted on powerful swells, the sheer rock walls of the narrow channel threatening on either side as the tug and barge careened through the slot.

And then we were through, and the world became instantly tranquil. We cleared the decks, let the dogs out, and I made a pot of much anticipated coffee.

Skip had been looking for a permanent mate for months. Finding good people was a problem shared by even the big tugboat companies. Skip was thrilled when he heard from Jerry Jensen, and signed him on as mate in March 1994. He had worked for Skip years before on the Magic, and had gone on to be skipper for Alaska Transport for years.

He was tired of going to Alaska, and wanted to relax and find a sailboat to live on. Having Jerry on board was a real pleasure. He was steady, knowledgeable, easy going, and willing to help with the ongoing work on the tug. Jerry had done a lot of painting on the Alaska Transport boats, and he jumped right into our project of painting the Michael's pilot house and stack. Skip liked to give him a bad time about the incident on the Magic when he fell into the bilge and was clobbered on the head by a deck plate that Jerry had moved.

With Jerry as mate, we began another dredge tending job for A.H. Powers, in July of 1994, this time at Kenmore on the north end of Lake Washington. The Michael was taller than the Magic and, unlike the Magic, her mast did not fold down. This meant that we had to have the Fremont Bridge raised for us every time we came through.

One early evening we were coming from Kenmore with the loaded dump scow on our way to Elliott Bay. While still in Lake Union, Skip contacted the bridge tender and arranged for an opening. The bridge tender told him to keep coming and he'd have the bridge up by the time we reached it. Jerry and I stood at the bow where we could see Skip in the wheelhouse, and we watched the bridge. Cars were stopped all along the span, with nobody moving. Skip reduced the Michael's speed and called the bridge to find out what was going on. He was told there had been an accident on the bridge. Skip asked him why he didn't let him know. The bridge tender said "Oh, I thought you knew."

We were entering the approach to the bridge where the lake ends and the canal starts. Skip had to make a hard turn to port, powering the barge loaded with 2,000 tons of dredge spoils, around putting tremendous strain on the tow wire and bridles. Jerry and I went aft to keep an eye on the towline, our stomachs in knots as Skip turned the tug and barge around and took us back into Lake Union to wait for the bridge to be cleared, and to allow our adrenaline levels to ease back to normal.

Where there is a low bridge blocking passage of large vessels, the skipper has to rely on the judgment of the bridge tender. It can lead to uneasiness in the wheelhouse, because timing is critical and options are minimal in the confines of a channel.

On a trip to Tacoma, Skip requested an opening of the Hylebos bridge so that he could continue up the Hylebos waterway from Commencement Bay. The bridge opened and he started through the uprights with the Magic when one half of the bridge span crashed down, just missing the pilot house with Skip at the wheel.

Low bridges aren't the only hazard. One day on the way to Steilacoom, the Magic was going under the Tacoma Narrows Bridge when someone dropped a plank down on them, just missing Myron, the mate, who was out on deck. On another occasion someone flipped a lit cigarette off a bridge into a dusty (chip barge) that Skip was towing. It smoldered for a time and then burst into flames.

One trip we made to Jervis was in beautiful summer cruising weather. We were in the wheelhouse having our after dinner dessert and coffee enjoying the beauty of the Strait of Georgia as we moved north, with the city of Vancouver to starboard. From our vantage point on the strait, we could see the mountains behind the city rising dramatically, as well as the mountains on Vancouver Island to the west. The scenery and the ethereal evening light were nothing less than stunning.

There were a few pleasure boats out, taking advantage of the long days to make a few more miles before finding moorage for the night in one of the many bays and inlets among the islands along the edge of the strait.

The VHF radios were dialed in to channels 16/13 and Vancouver Traffic, which monitors ship movements in the strait. They are very efficient, keeping radio transmissions to a minimum. The ensuing quiet in the wheelhouse after switching over to Vancouver Traffic is a big relief from Seattle Traffic, which can be an incessant barrage of irritating noise.

We heard someone call Vancouver Traffic and say "This is Billy's Dream." Vancouver Traffic acknowledged. The male voice asked Vancouver Traffic if they could tell him where he was. Seeing that this might be a lengthy conversation, Vancouver asked him to switch to a

THE PITT RIVER QUARRY AT A WIDE SPOT IN THE RIVER. THE TUG IS AT THE DOCK IN THE MIDDLE OF THE PICTURE.

RIDING OUT HURRICANE FORCE WINDS IN BOOM BAY, TIED TO A LOG RAFT.

different channel. This sounded entertaining, so Skip switched over to listen. With darkness just a few hours away, Billy's Dream seemed to not have a clue where he was, in even the most general terms. As we listened to him speak, we began to hear the fuzziness in his pronunciation, and it became apparent that he was quite drunk. Without any information to go on, Vancouver Traffic could do nothing for him. If Billy's Dream was a fiberglass boat, which was probably the case, it would hardly make a blip on the radar screen. He hailed Vancouver several more times that evening, each transmission increasingly slurred. We wondered how long he would last out there among the many rocks and swift currents.

The next morning, Skip came into the galley to get a cup of coffee. He said "Guess who I heard on the radio just now?" Billy's Dream had made it through the night and, from the sound of it, the liquor supply was holding out, because he had obviously had a few nips at the bar already. He wanted to know if Vancouver Traffic had figured out where he was yet.

In September of 1994, Jerry took a couple of weeks off, and Skip called his old friend, Les Baker, who had been on the Sea Imp and the Elk II with him, and asked if he could make a few trips with us. Les said that might make for an interesting change, and agreed to fill in for two weeks.

Our next job took us to British Columbia. At 04:30 in the morning we were abeam of Sand Heads, which is the entrance to the Fraser River. Around the mouth of the Fraser are miles of tide flats, through which has been dredged a five mile long channel. The entrance to this channel is marked by a 101' tall Texas tower, which is visible for miles out in the Strait of Georgia. The channel into the river is very well marked with lights, as is the Fraser itself. Each bend in the river is marked with a quick flashing light, which is easily distinguishable from the rest of the navigation aids.

As the Michael followed the river inland with the barge in tow, the sun rose over the busy waterway, with New Westminster on the northern bank, beyond which was a wide bend to the right. On we went until the river narrowed because of an island in the middle, and we stayed left, taking the skinniest channel and continued left at another fork in the river. We were now in the Pitt River, smaller and shallower than the Fraser. From the river banks protruded docks, boat houses, and log storages, which choked the navigable part of the river down to a scrawny stretch of water. In a 102' tug, with a 45' wide by 180' long barge, it seemed nightmarishly constricted.

At an angle to the river, we encountered a railroad bridge which, when closed, is low over the river and must be raised to allow passage of a vessel of Michael's size. Once through that bridge we came to another bridge which sat cattywampus across the river. This bridge is always closed because it is used by cars, so Skip had to request an opening with the bridge tender. He had it open for us as the Michael slowly bucked the current, and then Skip opened the throttles and we slid through at a pretty good clip. Navigation through logs and sandbars soon occupied the attention of everyone on board as the river snaked around and became impossibly thin in width as well as in depth. Then up ahead there was a wide, lazy bend, and in that open area we saw the rock quarry, and we were soon tied up to the dock.

Skip had brought the Magic up the Pitt River a number of times, and I had made the trip before, but this was the first with the Michael. With her extra ten feet of length, four feet of width, and two feet of depth, she seemed much too big for the river. The tugs that were designed for work on the Fraser were small with shallow drafts.

The Pitt is a messy river strewn with logs and debris. We saw many small runabout sized boats on the river, and everyone had a line around a big chunk of wood that they were towing behind them.

It took the crew at the pit ten hours to drop enough large rocks onto our barge. With the boat tied alongside the barge, we got to hear every single one of them land. Getting any sleep was impossible, but it was a sunny, warm day and we relaxed on the Michael's aft deck. While we waited, Skip took me to the office to meet, Bob, the cat. When we opened the door, I could not help but see this huge animal; he had to be a Maine Coon cat. The people at the quarry had noticed him lurking at the edge of the woods every once in a while, and had begun putting out food for him because he looked like he was trying to survive on his own. Over time they had gained his trust, and he had been coaxed into the office where everyone enjoyed his amiable personality. When I met him, he was extremely affectionate and liked to be picked up and held, which was a real weight-lifting exercise.

It was dark by the time the barge was loaded. If negotiating the Pitt River in the daylight with an empty barge is tense, doing it at night with a loaded barge seems sheer folly. The trip down the Pitt was accomplished with one person at the spotlight, playing its beam over logs and obstructions in the murky water. Another person followed our progress on the long chart with their finger, with Skip steering and giving directions, and everyone peering anxiously into the night. The chart for the Pitt River is a long, two page affair. An hour and forty minutes after leaving the dock we were at the railroad bridge.

An infrequent visitor, without local knowledge, has a difficult time figuring out the tidal influences accurately, this far up the river. There is an ebb and flow in the river, the calculation of which helps a skipper use the movement of the current, rather than having to fight it, especially in weaving a heavy barge through the bridges. The railroad bridge looks intimidating because it is approached at an angle to the current, and the shear walls on each side are quite high. With the tug and barge being dragged downstream, the set up for getting through without bouncing off of anything must be done with a sure hand at the helm. The bridge tender sits in a little house above the shear wall, to port when heading down river. He is so close that the skipper can chat with him at normal volume as he goes by.

Once past the railroad bridge, we all began to breathe more easily. Out of the dark we saw opposing traffic; headed upriver a small runabout full of noisy people shot past us in the debris filled water, towing a water skier.

We were back at Sand Heads at 01:45 A.M., the Michael's bow pushing into the placid waters of the strait. As the sun began to erase the stars, we slipped into the San Juan Islands, the smell of freshly perked coffee permeating the boat. We passed islands bathed in oblique amber sunlight, the water and sky a deep turquoise. All of the doors were flung open and hooked to let in the fragrant warmth of the day. We delivered the loaded barge to Tacoma the next morning, and ran light back to Seattle.

A day later, we ran to Tacoma and picked up the empty barge for a trip to Jervis Inlet. At midnight we entered Rosario Strait in the San Juans, and it wasn't long before we were into thick fog. To complicate matters, there were fishing boats in the area with nets deployed in the strait. Even if they had lights on the ends of their nets, it wouldn't do us any good in the soupy conditions. About that time, there was trouble in the engine room. Skip throttled back to run down and see what was wrong. He shut down the starboard engine and we continued on, using the port engine. He left Les and me in the wheelhouse, huddled over the radar, trying to detect little blips that might be fishboats, as well as deciphering the outline of the islands, and the positions of buoys, as we groped our way through the islands. Skip worked for hours, repairing the engine while Les and I remained glued to the radar screen. Eventually, we started to see vague shapes out the windows and shortly after that we blew off the last tendrils of mist, happy to see that we were where we thought we were, with a reassuring buoy light blinking ahead of us.

Two days after the completion of that job, we departed Seattle with the barge and headed north to Lummi Island, at the upper end of the San Juans. We were off of Port Townsend as the sun began to set, coloring the sky a blazing magenta, and over Whidbey Island a big, orange harvest moon rose in counterpoint to the ongoing sunset.

Skip took us through another wall of fog in Rosario, which lingered around us as Skip made the turn at the north end of Guemes Island, that would take us to the east side of Lummi. It was very dark along that shore, where the land rises to 1740'. The quarry had no lights, so it felt like we were entering a black hole when the tug turned into a recess in the steep shoreline. The tug's deck lights and spotlight glowed back at us from two small reflectors on pilings near the loading area. The barge had to be spun around in the dark, lines made up quickly from the tug to the barge, and then slid into position and tied so that heavy equipment could bring rock aboard in the morning.

By 04:00 A.M. the barge was made fast, and Skip shut down the main engines. After hours of listening to the clamor of big engines, the muffled rap of the generator was almost soothing. We took advantage of the quiet to grab a few hours of sleep before boulders started dropping onto the deck of the barge.

When we stumbled out on deck later, with cups of coffee, the little cove had been transformed by the soft September light into a place of beauty. Beyond the low rocks at the entrance, sparkled the deep blue of Bellingham Bay. We appreciatively breathed in air smelling richly of warm fir trees.

We departed with the loaded barge at 12:50 P.M. and proceeded south for Everett, through a splendid afternoon. Had it not been for more engine trouble, it would have been an enjoyable trip.

In the ten months that we had been running the Michael, Skip and I had changed four heads, a liner, two pistons, rods, and bearings. In the two weeks that Les was on board, we changed four heads, two on each engine, as well as a piston, rod, and bearings.

We would pull into Everett and hand off the barge to a smaller tug that would take it up the river, and then, hours later, bring it back to us for another run to Lummi Island. Between runs, we would work in the engine room. The weather was the finest that September has to offer. It was hot at the dock where we were tied in Everett.

The port engine was starting to slurp water like crazy. Each engine had its own water tank with a sight gauge, and I was giving that engine a drink every hour that we ran. Skip found water in a cylinder, and further investigation showed that we needed to change two heads. There was not enough time to get it all done before the tug, Port Susan, brought the barge back to us and we had to leave for Lummi. So we went north using the starboard engine. We pulled into the Lummi pit at 02:00 A.M. and slept while the engine room cooled so that Skip could finish the repairs. By the time the barge was loaded, Skip still had a couple of hours of work left on the second head replacement, so we had to go on just the starboard engine again.

We had made it through the San Juans, and were off of Point Partridge at about six that evening when the engine room alarms went off. Skip shut down the engine then came topside to watch the barge as it kept moving, and we drifted for a while until the tow wire sagged to the bottom and anchored us in the shallower waters around the point. There was no choice but to go down and finish the head installation on the port engine.

The setting was utterly tranquil. There was no swell and there was not even a tickle of wind to mar the smooth surface of the water. Les and I watched the evening sky turn a mellow, ripe cantaloupe color, which infused the still water around us. At about 8:00 P.M., Skip fired up the port engine, and we completed our trip to Everett in the early morning hours. After a few hours of rest, Skip tore down the number three head on the starboard engine, and replaced the piston, rod and head before the next trip.

Inlet Marine tugs had towed the 180' barge, DTB-27, many thousands of miles over the years. It was a docile, well-behaved barge unless it had water in its hull, which would cause it to tow somewhat erratically.

With yet another new mate on board, on our first trip since Jerry Jensen left to go cruising in March of 1995, we picked up the DTB-27 for a trip to the Lummi Island quarry. The front fence at the bow of the barge had been removed. The fence is there to deflect water coming over the bow when the barge is loaded and plowing through waves. Skip complained to the customer that without the fence the barge's seaworthiness was compromised. They told Skip not to worry about it, they'd used it that way before.

We took the barge, with two big yellow front end loaders aboard, up to the quarry at Lummi where she was loaded with large rocks and a pile of smaller rocks. One of the loaders was positioned at the bow. As we headed for the Duwamish River, the wind picked up and we had a moderately rough crossing from Point Partridge to Point Wilson off of Port Townsend. We commented that, jeez, they must not care about their machinery, as we watched spray from the bow of the barge drench the loader. Sea conditions moderated as we entered Puget Sound. At midnight, after several uneventful hours, Skip turned the helm over to the mate, and went below to his room to get some sleep.

About forty-five minutes later, the mate roused Skip and told him he couldn't see the barge lights all of a sudden. Skip ran up to the pilot house and turned the searchlight back at the barge. All we could see was a smooth, dark shape low in the water. The barge had flipped over and dumped its load. The towing bridles had fallen off and the barge was adrift. We brought in the tow wire and went back to the capsized barge. It wasn't easy to put a heavy line on the upside down barge and have it remain in place or, for that matter, locate the bitt under water.

After a couple of tries we had a hold of her and put tension on the line to keep it from slipping off. Then we towed it at two and a half knots to the A.H. Powers dock in the Blair Waterway in Tacoma. Skip had called ahead to let them know what had happened. A crew was standing by when we arrived many hours later. They took advantage of the situation and did some work on the bottom and gave it a coat of anti-fouling paint before righting the barge. We never saw that mate again.

The following September we were making a trip into Jervis Inlet with the Michael and the barge from hell. We were enjoying sunny, shirt-sleeve weather as we left the San Juans behind. As we approached the Canadian border, we saw a cluster of small boats in the distance off of Point Roberts. This is a popular fishing spot for commercial and sports fishermen alike.

Continuing north, Skip noticed a man standing and waving his arms in a small, yellow runabout. He was alone in the boat, and was separated from the flotilla of fishing boats closer to shore. It looked like he was having engine problems, and was starting to drift farther out into the Strait of Georgia. Skip called us to the wheelhouse and told us that we were going to try to help this guy. We had only one shot at it because we had the barge strung out 1600' behind us, limiting our maneuverability. The mate and I each grabbed pikepoles as Skip made a course change in toward the beach, and throttled back.

Roberts Bank is part of the extensive mud flats that envelop the mouth of the Fraser River, some twelve miles to the north of Point Roberts. The little boat didn't have much farther to drift before being in the shipping lanes, in the path of large ocean going ships, as well as in the way of ferry traffic. The Tsawwassen ferry terminal, which had been carved out of the mud, was just three miles north of Point Roberts.

Skip nosed the 102' Michael gently alongside the 17' boat, her bow overshadowing it for a moment as she eased past. The crew walked along the deck, keeping pace with the small boat, as the man below held up his mooring line to us.

We walked the little boat back along the port side to the aft deck, which afforded the easiest boarding because of its relatively low freeboard. We tied the boat alongside and gave the man, who looked like he was well into his seventies, and was wearing waders, a hand up onto the Michael.

We asked him if he was alright, and he assured us that he was. I poured him a cup of coffee and led him up to the wheelhouse to see Skip, who was studying the water. The expanse of shallows stretches as much as five miles out from shore, and ranges from zero to two fathoms at low tide. The edge of this area was unmarked except for the Tsawwassen ferry landing. With the Michael's 11' draft, Skip did not dare to get closer to the beach.

As we discussed how we were going to get the man back to shore, we saw a pleasure boat coming from the north, on a course that would take it across our bow. Skip hailed the 30' boat on the radio, and explained our predicament. In response, the boat swung around and closed in on us as we moved slowly north, parallel to the shoreline. The mate and I helped the man down into his boat and we tossed his lines back to him, then we gave him a push with our pikepoles as the Michael fell away from him. When we had established some distance from him, the thirty-footer came in and picked up the bow line from the elderly man, and headed in to shore.

Once they were clear of us, Skip altered course for deeper water. By this time, the barge from hell was grazing aimlessly on the slack tow wire, so I concentrated on keeping the wire from snagging anything on the aft deck as Skip increased the Michael's speed. We had just taken strain on the tow wire, and our attention was still focused aft when we saw a substantial splash back by the barge. There was a series of splashes, each one closer. Skip had seen them from the wheelhouse, and walked aft on the boat deck. We looked at each other and said "You don't suppose it could be …."

We watched with delight as a whale pulled up on our port side and stationed itself alongside the aft deck. He swam along with us for about twenty minutes. What was truly marvelous was that this whale had visited us before. On that occasion, we had been across the strait from Tsawwassen, around Active Pass, traveling south with a loaded barge. Because we had been going more slowly, the whale had stayed with us for about forty-five minutes, taking up the same position on the port side.

We had been absolutely thrilled by the whale's visit. We had thought it was a once-in-a-lifetime event. We had worried about it because we had read that whales are social animals. Why was this one alone, and what kind was it? Was it sick? For weeks we talked about it. So here he was again, looking great.

Dusty went nuts, acting the same way she did when porpoises would show up to play in our bow wave. She barked and tore around on deck, and threw her front paws up on the bulwarks for a look, and then she'd run in circles on the deck again.

Any time the Dall's porpoises came to play, they were always wonderfully entertaining. We might spot them a mile or two away, and before long they would zoom on over to the tug for a bit of sport. Watching them from the bow was to witness pure, unrestrained joy. They pulsed through the curling wave, sleek torpedoes of dynamic energy. Their presence was always a very moving experience.

On a mid-December day in 1995, we departed from the ship canal with the barge from hell, at ten in the morning headed for Tacoma. We came out past the Shilshole entrance buoy and Skip checked in with the Vessel Traffic System (called Seattle Traffic). We headed south, staying close to the West Point buoy, intending to stay east of the traffic lanes

SKIP AND THE WHALE WE FIGURED WAS A PILOT WHALE. SKIP NAMED HIM PONTIUS.

THE WHALE SWIMMING ALONG WITH US, AND THE BARGE FROM HELL MEANDERING ALONG BEHIND.

until Three Tree Point.

It was a filthy day, achingly cold and raining, with visibility two miles and very fuzzy around the edges. We were taken by surprise to hear Seattle Traffic advising a couple of southbound tugs with tows that there was a sailboat race in progress.

We saw two boats sailing northwest into the murk. For some inexplicable reason there were quite a few pleasure boaters out on the sound as well. I remarked several times as I wiped condensation from the pilot house windows, that I couldn't understand why anyone who didn't have to would be out on a miserable day like this.

On our way across the mouth of Elliott Bay, unable to see the light at Alki Point as visibility deteriorated, we heard the Seaspan Liberator, a container ship, talking to Seattle Traffic as he rounded Point No Point for Tacoma, doing nineteen knots. Seattle Traffic advised him that there was a sailboat race in his path in the area around VTS buoy, Sierra Foxtrot, two miles south of his position.

We continued south as visibility worsened and rain beat on the wheelhouse windows, giving us visibility problems inside as windows fogged, as well as out. We listened for further transmissions from the Seaspan ship because he would be overtaking us at some point, and Skip wanted to be prepared for that by crossing the traffic lanes before he reached us. It wasn't long before we heard him on the radio.

"Seattle Traffic, this is Seaspan Liberator."

"Liberator, Seattle Traffic, go ahead."

"Traffic, are these people aware that they are supposed to stay clear of commercial vessels in the traffic lanes?"

"Liberator, yes, they've been informed of this."

"Well some blockhead with a blue star on his spinnaker just tacked in front of us and we had to maneuver to avoid him."

"Liberator, can you see his sails?"

"Yes, I can."

"Can you get the number for us?"

"Traffic, I would be more than happy to … "

"Seattle Traffic, this is Seaspan Liberator the number is ------ . This was the number on his spinnaker."

"Seaspan Liberator, thank you. We'll take care of it."

Fiberglass boats do not show up well on radar; a small unremarkable dot on the screen. On that day there was clutter from squalls on the radar throughout the day, making it even tougher to detect small boats. Owners of such vessels would be interested to hear conversations in pilot houses of tugs and ships bearing down on them, as binoculars come out and the water ahead is scanned. In conditions such as we experienced that day, we would make a sighting when the boat was about three-quarters of a mile away. That doesn't give a skipper much time to react when he's in a ship doing nineteen knots.

In December we were trying to make as many trips to Jervis as possible before the Lakeside plant shut down for a month after Christmas. On December 10, we left at ten in the morning reassured by a weather forecast that indicated no major disturbances. We had a consistent twenty knot southeasterly all the way to Point Partridge, switching to easterly twenty in the San Juans and the Strait of Georgia. The barometer had dropped slowly over the day and night as we made our way north.

We pulled into the pit at Jervis at 07:30 A.M. and had our load of gravel by 10:40. On our way south, a new and very different weather forecast was issued. A storm with hurricane force winds was building, and was expected to hurl itself at the Pacific Northwest. By the time we were halfway through the San Juans at 02:00 A.M. on the 12th, the barometer had fallen to 29.25. When we reached Burrows Island, just before 07:00, it read 28.90.

I gathered up all of the survival suits, and looked over each one, making sure the lights on each one worked, and that the zippers operated smoothly. Then I distributed the bright orange suits around the main deck, so that they would be within easy reach, making sure that there were enough for the two dogs. Then I double checked to make sure that all of the hatches were secure.

The storm struck Oregon first. In the wheelhouse, Skip listened to weather reports and news broadcasts of one hundred-plus mile an hour winds ripping roofs off of buildings around Portland.

THE BARGE FROM HELL, LOADED, ZIGZAGING ITS WAY HOME LIKE A DOG ON A LEASH, BEHIND THE MICHAEL.

THE DOGS WOULD COME TO THE MICHAEL'S ENGINE ROOM DOOR TO TELL US IT WAS TIME, ACCORDING TO THEIR CLOCK, FOR US TO KNOCK IT OFF AND GET THE HECK OUT OF THERE.

We rounded Point Partridge and crossed over to Port Townsend, the wind southeast between ten and twenty knots. At Marrowstone Island, the wind stilled and the barometer read 28.72. A muted, sepia light emanated from a sky full of strange clouds. We looked out at a world that resembled an old photograph.

Skip kept up with the progress of the storm, filling me in from time to time. We reached Point No Point at 2:25 in the afternoon, and the barometer read 28.60. Off of Kingston we were finally assaulted by the leading edge of the storm.

Three hours later we were at Shilshole Bay, shortening up the tow wire in building seas. It was much too wild to try to make up to the barge alongside, so Skip took it through the locks on the tow wire. The wind assailed us with a banshee screech as we approached the locks; the attendants on the wall above taking the full brunt of it. As we rose to the fresh water level, the piles of gravel acted as large sails against which the fury of the storm shoved mightily.

Once we cleared the guide walls of the locks, we had to perform a tricky maneuver to bring the barge into Lakeside's plant. The tug needed to be on the barge's port side. To accomplish this, the mate had to climb onto the bow of the barge and remove each towing bridle, which I pulled back aboard the tug, then he took the stern line I handed across to him and put the eye on the barge's bitt that the bridle had just come off of. Then Skip peeled off with the tug, leaving the barge loosely attached for a few minutes as he spun the tug and came alongside the barge. I had to tend the slack on the stern line so that it wouldn't get sucked into the propellor. I then walked quickly forward to hand the spring line over to the mate who had gotten in position on the barge to accept the spring line and get it over a designated bitt near the midpoint of the tug.

All the while, the wind was insistently pushing the barge, and the mate with his artificial leg wasn't fleet of foot on his best day, and had to slog through gravel to tend the lines. We made the spring line fast and then both moved in the direction of the Michael's bow. The next line to go on was led from the bow of the tug to a bitt twenty feet beyond that on the barge. It was a stout, heavy line, and I had to hand it across to the mate who had to drag it while trudging over gravel, and drop the line's eye on the bitt. As he made his way back to the boat, I took several turns with the line around the drum of the bow winch and led the tail of the line to a cleat at the bow.

During this exercise, the wind continued to set us down at an alarming pace on a marina that is tucked behind the locks. The mate, at this point, needed to be back aboard the boat so that we could cinch up the bow lines with the winch and then run back to the stern and take up the slack in that line with the aft capstan, and make it fast. The point of all of this effort was to bring the boat in snugly to the barge so that Skip would be able to steer the barge with the tug. By the time we were done, having cast a few furtive glances at the rapidly approaching marina, Skip had his hands full bringing the bow up into the wind, using everything those cantankerous old engines had, to claw back around, away from the marina and head up the ship canal.

As we pulled away from the locks into the wind, a tour boat all decorated for the Christmas cruises came at us on our side of the canal. Skip blew a passing signal, but they did not respond. Skip then blew the danger signal, and they finally moved over to their side of the canal. With the wind blasting against the barge, trying to turn it sideways, Skip kept it under tight control with the tug.

We were gathered in the wheelhouse as we went up the ship canal. We heard the tour boat call the lock master to say they would be using the large locks. The lock master came back to them and said it would be best if they used the small locks because it would be safer for the lock attendants who were afraid they would be blown off the lock wall into the water.

We heard another tour boat call the Montlake Bridge and ask for an emergency opening so that they could go to Kirkland, a place that would have been wide open to the force of the storm. Even the floating bridges were closed.

The engine room log for the Michael brings to mind the saying "It's always something." On the trip in March 1995 when the barge capsized, the port engine overheated and had to be shut down. Skip changed a head at the end of the trip. In April the port engine overheated again and we changed another head.

After being on the Michael for a while I came up with the theory that the engines conspired with each other, something like "Hey, I think I'll take the next trip off." On the next April trip the starboard engine started drinking half a day tank of water an hour, with steam coming out of holes in the head covers; not something you really ever want to see. We had to shut down the starboard engine, give it the day off, because there was water in the lube oil. After the trip we changed a liner, piston, and rod.

In June we picked up the barge from hell in preparation for a gravel run to Jervis inlet. One of the starboard engine's cylinders was not firing, so we changed the nozzle. Two days later we headed for Jervis with the starboard engine gulping lube oil as fast as we could fill it. It was also back to drinking water like crazy.

In the three days before the next trip, we changed a liner, piston, rod, bearings, and heads. On June 10 the engine behaved itself all the way to Jervis. During the juggling to land the barge at the loading dock, the starboard engine began smoking, then started to vibrate badly, and it had to be shut down. It turned out that there was a badly worn spot on the crankshaft. On the trip back to Seattle we ran on the crabby port engine as Skip began dismantling the starboard engine.

We made a couple of shorter trips on just the port engine. In the meantime Skip and I took apart the starboard engine, replaced the crankshaft, and rebuilt the engine over a period of several weeks.

Almost a year to the day later, we were heading out with the barge using just the starboard engine because the port engine was in the midst of yet more work.

Skip was concerned about the generator on the starboard engine which had been acting erratically. Being a diesel-electric set up, the engine can't run without its generator. Skip asked me to go down and check on the generator setting, once he was done juggling and had the barge in tow.

When I opened the engine room door it looked like the Fourth of July down there. The generator was frying itself. It was toast. The

Skip guiding the crankshaft down the hatch.

The newly rebuilt Cleveland Diesel, freshly painted.

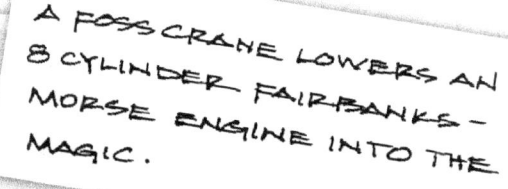
A Foss crane lowers an 8 cylinder Fairbanks-Morse engine into the Magic.

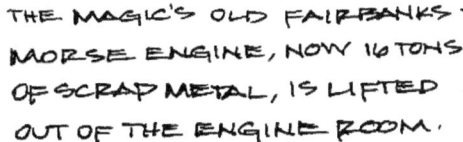
The Magic's old Fairbanks-Morse engine, now 16 tons of scrap metal, is lifted out of the engine room.

Magic's stack coming back aboard after the repower.

propulsion system that had caused us so much misery was a goner. We did not say any kind words over the deceased.

Before Skip could consider replacement for the worthless piles of junk in the Michael's engine room, we had to disassemble everything and hoist it out of the bowels of the boat. We hauled tons of metal to the recycling yard. The one good thing that came out of those old generators was a lot of copper. Skip and I spent months on this project, using the revenue from the metal recycling to fund our work.

As Skip checked out the various repower options available, one thing became abundantly clear. This would be an expensive endeavor. In the midst of trying out various financing strategies, Fred Dahl stopped by one day.

Fred's company, Dahl-Ferguson, had an eight cylinder Fairbanks-Morse engine that they had taken out of their tug, Neptune, and he offered to sell it to Skip. (We later found out that they had taken it out because they could never get it to run right). Skip had always loved the Magic, so the thought of bringing her back to life while we figured out what to do with the Michael was very appealing. It seemed like a fortuitous answer to the immediate dilemma. After marveling at this turn of events, we switched our efforts to the Magic. All we had to do was polish up our work ethic and tackle yet another engine room project. The old engine had to be detached from the boat; the top deck of the tug had to be cut out, and the sixteen ton piece of trash that was in there had to be hoisted out. The Magic was towed across the ship canal to the Foss Tug yard just a few hundred yards away, where a crane lifted the dead engine out to be sent to the scrap yard where it belonged.

A lot of work had to be done in preparation before the replacement engine could be installed. Plumbing for water and lube oil had to be reconfigured, and the engine bed had to be modified for the shorter engine. It was critical that the eight cylinder engine couple perfectly with the Lufkin reduction gear that turns the shaft to the propellor. With just two people doing the work, it took months.

When it came time to fire up the engine, Skip could not get it to start. He poured over the manuals, tried every Fairbanks trick he had ever learned over the years, and was dismayed that the wretched hunk of metal would not rumble to life. After weeks of tinkering and tweaking (this is when he found out about the previous trouble with this engine) smoke finally burped out of the stack. With the engine showing signs of life, back came the tow winch that had been moved to the Michael, as well as all of the heavy tools and equipment that we had hauled over there a few years earlier. By July 1999 Skip and the Magic were working together again.

After the repower was completed and the Magic had made a few trips for Lakeside, Skip brought her home. There were a few repairs he wanted to make, chiefly replacing a section of wasted steel in her transom. The Magic was moored off the beach in deep water between two dolphins.

Skip cut out a sizeable chunk of steel from the rake of her stern with an acetylene torch. He had new steel on the beach that he would cut according to patterns he had made. Each piece had to be small enough for him to put into the skiff and row out to the tug. He welded an eye into the middle of the steel plate so that he could hoist it into place with a piece of line and hold it while he tack welded the piece into the opening in the stern. Then he would row ashore and cut out the next piece from the pattern. He rebuilt the stern piece by piece in this manner. He sat in the skiff and welded it all back together.

It soon became obvious that smoke produced by this engine would be a new cause for head scratching. As Skip continued towing with the Magic, he racked his brain to come up with the solution to the smoking issue. Once the boat was pulling, the stack cleaned up quite a bit, but in the ship canal when the boat was at slow speed it was very noticeable.

And so it turned out to be the beginning of the end for Inlet Marine, a feisty little tugboat company. Skip made forty-one trips to Jervis Inlet before it became apparent that this was it for the Magic, with this engine. The EPA started fining him for emissions violations.

The old girl still had a blaze of glory left in her, though. In 2000 she was the honored boat at the Olympia tugboat races. She was featured on the promotional pins and posters, and she led the other tugs as they passed in review before the crowds of onlookers.

Because tugboating is a dangerous job made up of a lot of hard work and heavy lifting, it was decided in the late 1940s that a lighthearted

MAGIC, OLYMPIA TUGBOAT RACES, 1985.

social event that brought tugboats and their crews together would be just the thing. Hence, the idea of tugboat racing caught on and lasted until 1955. The idea did not rekindle until 1975 when Olympia began hosting these races, attracting more boats and spectators as the years went by.

The Magic kicked some butt at the 1985 races. At sixty-two years of age she had the best time overall in a field of thirty-four tugs, with nine minutes over a two nautical mile course. She set a more stately pace for her 2000 race with two bagpipers aboard playing jigs as the Magic plowed through the waters of Budd Inlet on her final romp as a working tug. She had made it to the new millennium.

Skip's days as an independent tugboat operator were over.

You can't keep someone who loves their work down, though, so Captain Lampman rode off into the aurora borealis on the tug, Billy H, with a dog at his side. But that's another story and another adventure.

BIBLIOGRAPHY

Edited by E.W. Wright & Gordon Newell. *H.W. McCurdy Marine History of the Pacific Northwest.* Seattle: Superior Publishing, 1966.

This tremendous reference work provided valuable details and clarification for the early chapters of the book.

www.ingramcontent.com/pod-product-compliance
Lightning Source LLC
Chambersburg PA
CBHW071729080526
44588CB00013B/1950